# PARENTING
## WITH RESPECT AND
# PEACE
# FULNESS

## LOUISE A. DIETZEL

*To Gail and Glenn*
*Love and Peace*
*Louise A. Dietzel*

STARBURST PUBLISHERS

P.O. Box 4123, Lancaster, Pennsylvania 17604

# PARENTING
## WITH RESPECT AND
# PEACE
# FULNESS

**LOUISE A. DIETZEL**

To schedule Author appearances write:
Author Appearances, Starburst Promotions, P.O. Box 4123
Lancaster, Pennsylvania 17604 or call (717) 293-0939

Credits:
Cover art by David Marty Design
Illustrations by Bill Dussinger

**PARENTING WITH RESPECT AND PEACEFULNESS**

First Printing, May 1995

ISBN: 0-914984-66-7
Library of Congress Catalog Number 94-067445
Printed in the United States of America

# This Book Is Dedicated To:

*Sam,* my spouse, best friend and partner in parenting, who, when I got scared, would be peaceful and assure me our children would make it in life in spite of us.

*Laurie,* our first born, who gave me the first opportunity to learn on-the-job what it was all about to be a parent, who experienced the brunt of my anxiety, and who, because of my inexperience in parenting, took responsibility that was mine.

*Rebecca,* our second born, who increased the on-the-job training, and who taught me that I had enough love for two children and that kids come with their own temperaments and personalities which require new learning of parents so they can respond to their kids' individualities.

*Beth Ann,* our third born, who gave me even more on-the-job training even though I thought I knew it all, who challenged me to redefine what was important, and who was closer to me because I was less anxious.

Thank you all for loving me as you have and for teaching me so many valuable lessons about being a parent. If I had a second chance, I would love myself more, allow you at an earlier age to do for yourself what you are capable of doing, not project my unmet needs and unfulfilled expectations onto you, and let you go freely.

## Acknowledgements

I am grateful to my parents, *Velma and Daniel Walter Miller* who gave me the gift of life.

I am grateful to *Sam, Laurie* and *Glenn, Rebecca* and *John,* and *Beth Ann* and *Kevin* for their support, encouragement, and love.

I am grateful to the parents and children who provided the experiences for me to learn and understand more about parenting.

I am grateful to my personal editor *Lois Friesen,* Professor of English, who helped me to grow as an author.

I am grateful to *David A. Robie,* Vice-President and *Ellen Hake,* Editor-in-Chief of Starburst Publishers for accepting and believing in my manuscript.

# Contents

## To All Parents

May you have the courage to accept
your humanness and your history and to give
your children the greatest gift of all—loving yourself.

# Definition of Respect and Peacefulness

For this book two basic terms, respect and peacefulness, need definition. Respect is the process of genuinely valuing, regarding, esteeming, considering, accepting, appreciating, noticing, and honoring yourself and others. It is not conceit or arrogance. Respect can be present when there is disagreement or when you do not like your child's behaviors. Respect is the opposite of criticizing, excluding, hating, ridiculing, judging, censuring, rejecting, and blaming.

Peacefulness is feeling calm, tranquil, content, relaxed, serene, gentle, and centered within yourself. Peacefulness comes from accepting your birthright that states that you are a wonderful, complete, lovable, and valuable person who is entitled to fulfillment, happiness, and joy. Peacefulness is the opposite of conflict, violence, turmoil, tension, distress, agitation, and discontentment. Peacefulness comes from within you, not from others' behaviors.

My observation is that when respect and peacefulness are common denominators within and between parents and children, wonderful things happen, such as closeness, resolution of a power struggle, acceptance of differences, clearer communication, and deepening of love for each other. Respect and peacefulness are parents' greatest assets and parenting tools. Both begin within you and affect your parenting in profound ways. Teaching parents and children to give, value, and invite respectfulness and peace because you deserve respect and peacefulness in return from each other is my gift to you. This is the thesis of this book.

My wish is that any or all of this will be helpful to you, wherever you are in your parenting process. I share what I have learned from parents and children with you to enhance respect and peacefulness in your journey with your children. It is never too soon or too late to learn more about the most important job in your life and to experience more confidence, respect, and peace.

# Preface

This book has evolved from four important roles I live: fifty-six years as a person, thirty-four years as a spouse, thirty-one years as a co-parent of three lovely daughters, and twenty years as a professional counselor and psychologist working in the public school system and in my own private practice. All are significant and invaluable experiences that have taught me so much. The interrelationships among these roles make it difficult at times to see the fine lines among them. What I do and learn in one area, affects me greatly in another area. All teach me about human behavior and the importance of respect and peacefulness.

In my counselor and psychologist role, I have the honor and privilege of listening and responding to children's and parents' concerns, frustrations, beliefs, wishes, dreams, pain, joys, and regrets. Even though each individual believes he/she is the only one who is feeling a certain way, I hear similar themes and struggles. For both parents and children, the commonalities are greater than the differences.

In addition to my counseling and therapy, I create and facilitate parent-training presentations and workshop series. Here my therapeutic relationships with children are helpful. Hearing both the children's and parents' experiences, I see the complete picture. The struggles and frustrations are not dissimilar. Frustration feels the same to a child as it feels to a parent. The obvious differences between them is the parents are older and have more responsibility than the children.

To me, the commonalities of the parents' experiences are greater than any differences:

- Fathers who have power struggles with children.

- Mothers who mistrust themselves and feel guilty.

- Fathers who are unsure of how to set clear limits reinforced with clear and reasonable consequences.

- Mothers who don't know exactly how much freedom and responsibility to allow first-borns.

- Parents who are uncertain about developmental stages and tasks and how to ease their children through them.

All of these typical and common situations present challenges, concerns, and questions for parents who are searching for seemingly elusive common denominators *Respect and Peacefulness.*

# Introduction

You as a parent are a very busy person. You find yourself in a job with no prior training except your childhood and your parents' treatment of you. You know what it is to be a kid and to relate to parents even though you might like to forget.

In your more honest moments, you can recall feeling overpowered by the BIG adults, not being heard when you had reasonable or strong feelings, being punished or treated unfairly, being told you do not know what you are talking about, and being preached at with the same lecture over and over. It was to the point you had it memorized and chose to modify your behavior to please adults even though you were not being true to yourself.

When you enter parenthood, the only training of any substance is on-the-job. Unlike repacking a box of tablets from the assembly line or throwing away the scoop of ice cream spilled on the floor and scooping a fresh one, the on-the-job-training is costly. Your effects which have more to do with learned, historical, behavioral patterns than with love or intentions are far-reaching and long-lasting. Being creatures of habit, you continue to behave in ways that were modeled for you even when you are not aware of the sameness.

The power, impact, and challenge of your parental influence and modeling supersede intentions, dreams, and promises made before parenthood. In other words, you as a parent are a very important person whose behavior affects your children even though you may not think it does. This can only be appreciated as you become a parent and experience what the role is about. At times, the magnitude of the role is appreciated by you and your child only when your child is grown. Needless to say, you have also grown up.

At this point, with many hours of on-the-job training, parenting wisdom and confidence have developed and increased. You wish there had been a faster way to learn this wisdom. Since this is the process, your children go on to be parents and struggle as you did to learn what it is to be a parent and create their own wisdom and parenting skills.

This book provides thought and insight through the summaries, text, examples, and suggestions about understanding and appreciating your role and function as a parent. Emphasis is given to the importance of *respect* and *peacefulness*. Since I have worked with many children in therapy, I have also included accounts of children's perceptions and experiences which complete the other side of parenting. As you understand and appreciate both of these, the opportunity is there to deepen acceptance of yourself and your children which can only increase your level of joyfulness and confidence. You deserve all the peace, respect, and self-reliance you can create, and so do your children.

The following rules can assist you.

## Louise's and Sam's Rules For Life

- I am responsible for and to myself.
- I create my own experiences and feelings.
- Each time I speak, I really am saying more about myself than I am saying about you, even though I attach your name to it.
- At any time, I am doing the best I can do.

My spouse Sam, also a psychologist, and I have worked together professionally with many individuals, couples, and families during the past twenty years. In our earlier work together, we learned that even though the presenting problems or concerns varied, our responses had the same themes: take charge of your thinking and reactions; change, rather than repeat, your history; understand personal boundaries and do not personalize what others say; and accept yourself without judgment and guilt.

We wrote the four rules from these themes and now share them freely with clients, friends, workshop and presentation participants. We hear that a good place to post them is on the refrigerator. Sam has graciously given me permission to print our rules in my book.

They are rules for life—living with yourself and others. Many aspects of your life have rules like driving a car, paying your rent, mortgage and taxes, playing sports, or getting an education. When you violate any of the previous rules, there are obvious consequences that follow. You know the consequences ahead of time.

The same is true for these rules of life even though the consequences might be less obvious.

The essence of the four rules is taking responsibility for yourself. Consequences from violating these rules are the following: loss of personal power, integrity, self-control, and self-responsibility; decreased self-esteem, self-respect, and peacefulness; increased responsibility that is not yours, and increased feelings of depression, anxiety, worry, guilt, and self-victimization.

These rules serve as the basis for this book and are frequently referred to either directly or indirectly.

The following is a brief explanation of each rule to familiarize you with them and to help you understand the examples more clearly in each chapter.

## I Am Responsible For And To Myself

You are responsible for you. This is true with what you choose to eat, drink, how much sleep and exercise you get, the level of stress you create and tolerate, and the care you give to your emotions. It is much easier to care for yourself physically, since those areas of need are more clearly defined, than emotionally.

Your emotional needs are less clearly defined to you since your feelings are so close to you. You live closer to yourself than anyone else. In fact, you can get stuck in your own feelings, which detract from your objectivity. Yet, whatever you think, feel, say, or do, in the final analysis, is your responsibility.

You are your own separate individual. This includes everything you believe, think and feel, how you react and behave, what you say or do not say, your behavior at all times, what is conscious and subconscious for you, and how you take care of yourself physically, emotionally, socially, and spiritually. If you blame others for how you think, feel, or behave, the costly consequence is that you give your personal control and power away to others, thereby, victimizing yourself.

This ground rule leaves no room for self-victimizing; victimization is not self-respecting or peace-enhancing.

## I Create My Own Experiences And Feelings

You continue to create your life, given what you have experienced in your lifetime to this moment. This includes what has been painful or joyful, loving or scary, supportive or destructive, fulfilling or disappointing, toxic or healthy, conscious or subconscious.

You are at the helm of your life-ship, giving the signals to yourself. The signals, what you say to yourself, might be the old and familiar ones you used as a child to survive traumatic or painful times, or to maneuver around your parents'/other adults' needs, or to get your needs met. The reason for understanding about the signals is not as important as knowing that the signals belong to you. Now, you are in charge of continuing to use them or letting go of them; you are in charge of changing the patterns of your own behavior. All are a part of your steamer trunk of beliefs, attitudes, feelings, and behaviors at this moment.

Again, this rule, like rule number one, does not support self-victimization. It excludes blame or attack on your parents or other significant adults who were surviving and doing the best they could. Perhaps those important adults did not love and respect themselves or know of their significance and impact on your life.

### Each Time I Speak, I Really Am Saying More About Myself Than I Am Saying About You, Even Though I Attach Your Name To It

You cannot speak for another person just as no one can speak for you. When you talk, you are saying what is going on inside you and what you are believing, thinking, and feeling even if you blame or verbally attack someone. Your perceptions, reactions, beliefs, and projections belong to you.

This is not to say that you are not affected by others' behaviors and reactions. It is knowing that others' reactions belong to them. As children, you were dependent on your parents' reactions and behaviors. Your life and survival created the need to cling to what they said and did. They were in control of you and the situation. Little did you know that they were talking about what was going on inside of them.

As you shift your focus from what they said or say to what you believe, think, feel, and do, you take more responsibility for yourself. This is never an easy shift, yet it is critical to your emotional well-being and taking charge of your life.

This rule, the most difficult of all to learn, safeguards the tendency to personalize (think and believe what the other person is saying is a statement about you) what others say, in addition to, allowing you to create your own personal, respectful boundaries.

## At Any Time, I Am Doing The Best I Can Do

It is easy to feel bad and berate yourself for not knowing earlier what you know now. Having intelligence and memories make it possible to recall what you knew at earlier times. You know the old adage well, "If I knew then what I know now . . . things would be different." You know how it would have been different. You know that you could have saved yourself some inner turmoil and emotional expense. There is nothing you can do about the past except to accept it, let it go, and to not repeat the same patterns if you deem those behaviors to be self-defeating.

The only moment you are sure of and have control over is the present moment. The past is gone and the future never comes. What you choose to do in any given moment is in your control. You may choose to incorporate a lesson or an awareness in the present moment from what you learned in the previous moment, thereby, making the future different from the past.

Given how each moment is fleeting with what is going on inside of you, you are doing the best you can do. If you could do it differently, you would. Beating yourself up in retrospect for what you did or did not do, only generates guilt. Guilt is a debilitating, counter-productive emotion that uses much of your time and energy. Your energies are valuable and can be used in better ways.

This is a ground rule to eliminate guilt, to teach letting-go of the past, and to teach self-forgiveness. Guilt and peacefulness are opposites.

All of these rules are simple, yet profound. Like so many aspects of your life, what is obvious and simple is overlooked and difficult.

You might find it helpful as you read each chapter to reread the ground rules. You cannot understand them too deeply or use them too much. Indeed, repetition is a great teacher.

If you decide to keep a parenting journal, write the preceding rules in the front of your journal and make entries as they make more sense to you in your everyday life with yourself and your children. Your time is always in great demand, yet you need to take time for you. I hope you will find a regular time to think, reflect, and write. A few minutes a day can make a difference—you and your children are worth it. You cannot afford to bypass the most important adult in your child's life—you.

# 1

# Being a Parent: Learning From Reflections of Your Childhood

## Introduction

Your childhood is your best resource for being a parent, be it primarily joyful or painful. Allowing your memory to revisit earlier times brings back specific historical scenes and situations that include: how old you were, how your physical surroundings looked, who was there, where your position was in the family, how you felt, what behaviors you learned to cope and survive, what and how your needs were met, what experiences were hurtful or comforting, and what was important to you and others.

Remembering what it was like to be a child at different stages of your development, while reflecting on what you experienced and felt, can keep you in tune with what your children might be experiencing. Recalling issues and situations that still feel unresolved can allow you the opportunity to bring resolution to these historic times.

Resolution is achieved in one of two ways. The first is by talking with the person(s) involved, if that is possible. If he/she is not alive anymore or are unavailable, the alternative or second way is to confront what you remember by talking about it with someone you trust who can help you to put the memories in the perspective as they occurred when you were a child. Keep in mind that as a child you felt powerless and dependent and were at the mercy of the adults.

For the first option, if the person(s) is available, tell him/her that you have some painful or haunting memories from your childhood that involve her, then ask if she would be willing to talk with you. It is possible that she is unaware of what you remember, or if she remembers, she needs to talk to you also, making amends and creating resolution for herself. If she is unwilling to talk, which is a statement about herself that might include denial, regret, shame, or guilt, at least you have prefaced your request to talk by telling her that you remember what happened. You can tell her, if she changes her mind and is willing to talk, to let you know. It works best when the person(s) involved is willing to talk. When that is not so, the second option is to deal with your memory without the other's direct involvement. Either way, the effects are greater for you than the other person since you live closer to yourself.

This second option includes understanding how old and dependent you were, what really was in your control, and guessing what was happening for your parent(s). Were they acting out how they had been treated by their parents? Were they dealing with stressful issues which put them on emotional overload? Were they out-of-control in their lives and, therefore, could not be there for you? Remember, when adults are not in charge of themselves, especially their greatest assets, peacefulness and respect, they project their neediness (unmet needs) onto their children. The result is that children take responsibility that is not theirs.

Resolution includes talking about the event(s) and expressing any stored feelings. Then, thinking from your adult perspective, you will probably arrive at one of the following conclusions:

- I was at the mercy of my parent(s)/other adults.
- I was young, dependent, and powerless.
- I did not do anything wrong.
- My needs, which were reasonable kid needs, were not met.
- I was abused and treated harshly. I deserved kindness.

- I was accused of something I did not do. I will not live with guilt for something that was not my responsibility.

- I was simply being a kid.

- My personal boundaries were violated.

- I took responsibility that was my parents. I can only take responsibility for me, not my parents no matter how much I love them.

All of these are accurate deductions giving you the break you deserved as a child and never got. Nevertheless, all are difficult conclusions, yet freeing for you. Difficult because, as a child, you took responsibility that was not yours and protected your parents, hoping in turn that your needs would be met. This belief is often carried into adulthood and requires hard work to change and maintain.

Given what happened to you, you may not be able to find resolution without the aid of a trusted friend, family member, or competent mental health professional.

For you, the benefit of resolution is letting go of the past baggage of hurts, losses, and unmet needs. Your task is to find the courage to confront the memories so that they do not continue (consciously or subconsciously) to take away your much needed energy, presence of mind, self-respect, and peacefulness.

Then, what follows and what you deserve are feelings of your own sense of freedom, allowing you to be more sensitive, open, available, loving, gentle, and understanding towards your children. By asking yourself the right questions, you can assist in the reflection process.

### → Ask Yourself These Questions

They will help with your introspection. Take time to think about each of them and trust the answers that come to mind. If you feel emotions that are intense, allow yourself to feel them and know that all of your feelings are all right.

1. Did you grow up with both parents? (If not, use adults in place of both parents.)
2. If not, who were the significant adults?

3. What is your earliest memory? What other memories do you have?

4. Is there a primary theme to your memories (pain, fear, joy, loss, rejection, abandonment, acceptance, peacefulness, anger, diminishment, guilt, responsibility)?

5. What trauma (unusual circumstances) did you experience (illnesses, hospitalizations, catastrophes, hardships, losses, accidents)?

6. To which parent did you feel the most closeness?

7. Is he/she alive today and if so what is your relationship with him/her? Has it changed since childhood and, if so, in what way?

8. Which parent did you go to when you wanted something important to you? What response did you receive?

9. Which parent disciplined?

10. What was the focus of his/her discipline (punish, revenge, take out frustration, criticize, teach lesson about your behavior, support, guide, remind)?

11. Were you punished? When? Who punished? For what?

12. What was your reaction (fear, rage, promise to get even or do better, submission, humor, panic, denial)?

13. Did your parents agree regarding discipline or punishment? If not, did you work one against the other?

14. How did you get attention (pouting, teasing, acting up, getting sick, being responsible, oppositional, defiant, cooperative, antagonistic, funny)?

15. What was the main way your parents connected with you (criticism, appreciation, judgment, guilt, approval, disapproval, threatening, acceptance, rejection)?

16. How did you get back or get even? What did you get in return?

17. As a parent, do you still behave in these ways?

18. How could you tell when your parents were upset? What did you do at these times?

19. Which parent was dominant and in charge in the family? In what ways and in what areas?

20. Who did you feel was most powerful, most controlling?

21. Which parent did you fear most? What did you fear?

22. Which parent did you respect most? What did you respect?
23. Were you loved conditionally or unconditionally? If conditional, what were the conditions?
24. If you had siblings, what was your relationship with them? Did your relationship change over the years? In what ways? If you were an only child, how did you feel about not having siblings?
25. What did your parents want for you and from you?
26. What thoughts are still with you from your childhood?
27. Which are positive, enhancing, respectful, scary, debilitating, defeating, guilt-inducing, enraging?
28. Which are gifts or punishments?
29. What hurts most from your childhood?
30. What have you done or are you doing to heal that hurt?
31. Who is in charge of you now?
32. What do you want for and from your children?

### → For Your Journal

Some of the questions will be easy to answer while others will take more thought. Make a journal entry of your responses. Be as brief or detailed as you wish. You can write your answer to each question, or write about the ones you find yourself thinking about most. Whatever your choice, write freely about your thoughts that emerge. Note how your answers change as you see your children grow and are reminded of your childhood. Go over the questions from time to time, and pay close attention to your answers whether they change or stay the same.

You might find it helpful to review the questions as your children enter new developmental stages and reach significant milestones. These could be walking, talking, first day-care, pre-school or kindergarten experience, first birthday party, sleeping away from home with or without parents the first time, first trauma, first communion or baptism, family trips, entering new schools, eighth grade and high school graduation, learning to drive a car and getting a license, first date, winning contests, illnesses or hospitalizations, and moves.

Memories that are vivid for you are conscious for you. What is conscious is in your control. On the other hand, what is subconscious for you is out of your awareness and feels like it is out of your control even though it affects your behavior. Periodic reflection on your childhood helps what is subconscious for you to become conscious and thus in your control.

As what you experienced as a child becomes conscious for you, you define clearer boundaries between your childhood and your child's childhood. The value of these boundaries is knowing what belongs to you. At some level, you relive your childhood when you have children. This awareness allows you to identify what was familiar or painful for you as a child, so you do not project the same onto your children.

## You Relive Your Childhood When You Have Children
When you have children, there is a predictable phenomenon that happens that is both conscious and subconscious. Since you have lived through your childhood and know what the role is about, you relive at both levels those earlier times in your thinking as your children grow. It is as though you see the child-part of you in bold, living color when you look at your children.

This is especially true when, as children, you felt extreme discomfort, fear, loneliness, powerlessness, rage, sadness, or guilt, and no adult assisted you in identifying, understanding, and expressing your feelings at the time. This same concept applies to the routine and familiar aspects of your childhood that were pleasant and joyful. When there are more times remembered filled with fear and anxiety than joy, the fear overshadows joy, and those feelings follow you to adulthood and parenthood.

Your task is learning to heal historical pain which includes loss, humiliation, disappointment, abuse, shame, and trauma, so it does not block how you see and relate to your children. It is defining respectful boundaries and knowing the pain belongs to you. As healing occurs, the tendency is lessened to project your pain onto your children. No easy task! You may have been able to do this on your own through reflection and introspection, or you may need to seek professional assistance.

## You Project Onto Your Children What Was Familiar or Painful For You as a Child

Your childhood has the tendency to limit and define you. It is your only experience and it is powerful. You can never fully understand or accept how all the individual situations and interactions from your childhood created your personality, beliefs, attitudes, behaviors, fears, tolerance, dreams, and survival mechanisms. It would take a video of your entire childhood, if that were possible, to make sense of your first eighteen years of life.

While you were critiquing and analyzing it, you would be missing out on critical events in your own and your children's lives. Being mortal does have its obstacles.

One example is that of a first-born son whose father was alcoholic and abusive. The son, a very sensitive person who felt sorry for his mother and three brothers, shielded them from their father's brutality by doing extra kindnesses for them and behaving in ingratiating ways. He put his own needs for a good father aside and was the good father to his brothers. At times, that meant taking the brunt of his father's out-of-control, abusive behavior.

When the son became a father, he vacillated between doing too much for his children (as he had protected his brothers) and feeling resentful toward his children because they were not doing enough for him (as his father had not done for him). His own familiar, painful, and unmet needs were displaced on his children.

The good news is as you become aware of what you missed, needed, or wanted in your childhood, you can take charge and either satisfy the wish or desire or let go of it. This is never an easy task; however, it is possible rather than impossible.

As a parent you will never meet all of the needs, desires, wants or wishes of your children. It just does not happen. You will never have all the awareness, skills, timing, energy, knowledge, understanding, answers, self-respect, and peacefulness. You develop these traits slowly as you gain experience in parenting. What you do not have does not negate the fact that you are a wonderful person—a fact that is your challenge to change into a strong, enduring belief.

In the example, the son who, when he became a father, found himself caught between his familiar behavioral patterns and wanting his needs from childhood met, had several choices:

- He could choose to mourn and grieve his loss of a good father, knowing he never would have a good father, in spite of the fact that he was deserving of a good father. Then, after a period of grieving, he could let go of ever having a good father.

- Or he could find a man who might be a good substitute father for him: sharing activities like playing golf, talking, fishing, refinishing furniture, or sharing coffee on Saturday morning. It would not be essential to share the intent of the relationship with the father-substitute unless there was much trust already developed. The primary gain would be for the man, needing a good father-son relationship experience, not for the substitute father.

- Or if his father is still living, the son could risk talking with his father about what the chances are of sharing life in a loving father-son manner. This risk would call for honesty and openness and would assess if his father has made the necessary changes needed to share in a different way than he was able to share in earlier years. Both of them would be beneficiaries of relating to each other with greater respect, integrity, and acceptance. Of course, if his father is not open to or available for a changed relationship, this is not a viable option.

- Or the last choice for him is to learn to treat his children in opposite ways than he was treated by his father, knowing he is the adult and his needs for fathering will not be satisfied. This choice, a challenging one, given the power of parental modeling, supports history that is changing and changed, not repeated.

Even though you are physically capable of being a parent, you are not assured of having the emotional capacity and maturity to respond to children's needs. In fact, juggling the meeting of your unmet needs and your children's needs often poses a challenge that spirals up and down as you and your children grow.

The four following examples from the lives of Marilee, Peter, Karen, and Arthur illustrate how they, in their own ways, relived their childhood when they became parents. You will also see how familiarity from their childhood was projected onto their children. Then, as each adult became aware of his/her childhood experiences, they related differently to their own children, allowing the children to be themselves.

## Marilee

Marilee was thirty-two and the proud co-parent of three healthy children: Amy, six; Sara, four; and Justin, two. Recently, Marilee felt extreme resentfulness toward Amy and was often critical of many things that she did. Intellectually, Marilee knew Amy was being a typical six-year-old, and Marilee could not make sense of her reaction toward Amy. Since Amy's birth, their relationship was close and pleasant with no more than the usual mother and daughter differences and squabbles that were quickly resolved.

As Marilee reflected on her childhood, she had fond memories that when she was four her father took her and her three-year-old brother to the local park. She recalled swinging on the swings, going down the long, yellow slide with a curve in the middle, getting a chocolate creamy from the ice cream vendor, romping in the grass that was full of clover and bees, feeding the pigeons stale bread from home, picking dandelions, climbing on the grey whale statue next to the merry-go-round, and riding on her father's shoulders as he bounced her in and out of the trees. Other recollections of her father were filled with the same affection and exhilaration.

When she was six, tragedy hit. Her father was killed instantly in a car accident and her heart was broken. She mourned his death with the rest of the family and continued on with life. Her wish was always that he would return to her and they could again romp in the park. As she grew, she knew this would never be. A favorite uncle, whom she dearly loved, spent time with her and her siblings which fostered pleasant memories. For Marilee, it could never replace the specialness she felt with her father for six, short, precious years.

As she reflected on her childhood, she realized her resentment toward her six-year-old daughter was coming from the fact that Amy had someone, her father, of whom Marilee had been deprived when she was the same age. Since this was conscious for her and in her control, it made sense, and her annoyance toward Amy disappeared.

### Peter

Peter was the father of seven-year-old Nate and twelve-year-old Thomas. Peter was recently promoted to general manager of a large department store where he has worked for twelve years. He had worked hard to deserve the new position. His wife was a buyer in the same store and also had proven to be a valued employee over the years.

Their combined income was substantial, and they dreaded income tax time. However, both sons benefitted from the affluence and the opportunity to play sports, musical instruments, attend summer camps, and travel extensively with the family.

When Thomas turned thirteen, Peter started becoming miserly and attempted to curtail activities his sons and wife were familiar with and loved. Naturally, this change drew reactions of shock, disbelief, and rage from his spouse and sons.

Peter and Nate were at odds with each other to the point that Nate was beginning to hate his father. Mealtimes were a constant battleground for complaining, criticism, and sarcasm.

With the aid of professional help, Peter painfully remembered the impact of his father's bankruptcy when Peter was in his early teens. He remembered how times for his family were tight, and as a result, tensions and stress were high and were released when the family was together for the evening meal. Spending had to be curtailed and necessities were scrutinized on the basis of need.

As this childhood situation with so many buried feelings became clearer to Peter, he acknowledged the stored emotional pain, released the pain, and was able to make amends with his family.

Ironically, as Peter shared his part in an open, honest way, his family responded with caring, cooperation, and understanding. (Openness and understanding invite the same from the other person.)

### Karen

For seven years Karen was a single parent of eight-year-old Christopher whose father left before his first birthday and had not contacted him since then. Even though Karen grew up with both parents, her father was quiet and passive, leaving her mother with the responsibility for the family decisions, especially concerning the children.

When Christopher was six, Karen met a man who enjoyed being with both her and her son. All three shared mutual interests, activities, and good times; eventually Karen and the man married. Christopher was elated to have a step-father and Karen shared the exuberance.

After the honeymoon, Karen felt increasingly jealous when Christopher initiated conversation or activities with his step-father. The very thing she so desperately wanted seemed to be turning sour. She found herself planning and maneuvering so she would be the primary adult.

In her reflections about her life, she became aware that she had no familiarity as a child of going to her father for anything important, and for a greater part of Christopher's life, she was the one he depended on for his needs. When there was no other significant adult in Christopher's life, no conflict existed for Karen. As this changed, even though it was a change she wanted, it caused much turmoil until she reflected on her childhood.

If she had not taken into account what she lived as a child and young mother, she might have sabotaged the relationship with the very person who loved her and whom she and Christopher deserved and loved.

### Arthur

Arthur grew up on a large midwest farm where, from an early age, he and his eight siblings worked hard in the house, barns, and fields. Despite their hard work, the family subsisted at poverty level. He was fifth in the birth order, had above-average intelligence, loved to draw and paint, and had excellent musical ability. He wanted more than anything to take piano, guitar, and singing lessons; however, the family budget could not afford such luxuries.

Even when he was old enough to work outside the farm, he gave much of his paycheck to his parents for essentials. Family sickness, drought, high mortgage rates, and day-to-day needs continued to drain the meager income throughout the years. They could not get ahead financially.

Arthur's dream of a musical career was sublimated by doing well in his school music classes, taking parts in musicals, and trading records and tapes with his friends. He promised himself that when he was an adult he would pursue his love of music.

At age twenty-five, he found himself living at home, helping with many responsibilities on the farm, and caring for his aging parents. Survival, again, was prevalent over his dream. Only after his parents sold the farm and moved to a retirement village, did he begin to feel the freedom of deciding what he wanted to do.

He enrolled in a two-year college program, majoring in accounting, believing that would assure him employment. Toward the end of his first year, he met a journalism student whom he dated for a year and then married. The fact that his wife was still a full-time student necessitated his working to support them and pay his college debt. Within the next six years, a son and daughter were born. Subconsciously, he was experiencing what he had gone through as a child and young adult.

When his son was eight and his daughter was six, he bought and reconditioned an upright piano, found a piano teacher, and signed up both children for lessons. At first, the newness of the piano in the family room, their competitiveness for practice time, and the sense of mastery they felt when they played a song that sounded like a song carried them for several months. As the novelty wore off, it was a constant battle to get them to practice, and Arthur began to feel like his hard-earned money was being wasted.

The tension in the household was so great one day after he had hounded his son over and over to practice that the son yelled at his father, "If you like it so much, why don't you play the piano!"

His son's poignant response struck a chord in Arthur that felt like his heart was being ripped from his body. He broke into tears and was able to say, "You are right, my son. I have always wanted to play the piano." Both father and son embraced and cried together. The power struggle ended.

Arthur knew he had recreated what was familiar for him as a child, and he owned the experience as his own. It was a dream from his childhood that, for reasons beyond his control, never came true and that belonged to him. The process of ownership gave him control that he did not have as a child. Consequently, he felt his own emotional freedom for the first time in many years; freedom that allowed him to take lessons and play the piano.

## What Are You Recreating From Your Childhood?

These accounts from the lives of Marilee, Peter, Karen, and Arthur exemplify how familiarity from their childhood experiences was reactivated when their children became the same age each of them had been. The ground rules, especially the second one, **I create my own feelings and experiences,** undergird the four situations.

As an adult, you are the only one in charge of your unmet needs and unfulfilled expectations. You are not powerless and dependent anymore except as you believe you are. You determine your sense of powerfulness or victimization.

As difficult as it is to make this switch from believing your parents (or any other adults you see as powerful and authoritative) are still responsible for you, especially as it relates to your emotional well-being, it is vital to shift the focus to the control you have. Initially, this shift occurs in your thinking by what you say to yourself, in addition to how much you believe what you say to yourself. Thinking you have little or no control in your life and are powerless, supports that belief. What you think is more belief than fact.

Saying rules one and two over and over again, until you believe them, is a way of making this shift from dependency to independency.

**I am responsible for me. I create my own feelings and experiences.** In certain ways, you become a parent to yourself and this continues through your lifetime. You take charge of your needs, wishes, wants, and desires just as parents are in charge of meeting their children's needs. Often it is easier to recognize your children's needs than it is your own.

For instance, suppose you have taken time to plan a special birthday party for your ten-year-old daughter that includes decorating with her favorite colors, inviting her special friends, playing games she enjoys, and letting her choose the menu. After the party, which everyone, especially your daughter, enjoyed, you feel a let-down from the excitement and all of your hard work, and you need recognition and appreciation. You may feel resentful if your daughter and her guests do not give you the thanks that you earned. There is a difference between what you earned, need, want, and deserve and what you receive from others.

To know this difference affords you another option. The choice to reflect on the gifts that you gave of your creativity in planning, sensitivity to her tastes, time to prepare for and be a hostess during the party, and your combined effort and energy to make her birthday party a memorable and special event. In this way, you take charge of what you need and give it to yourself. What you get from knowing this concept is increased psychological freedom and independence.

The only other option is to blame, criticize and judge, and therefore diminish your children or your parents with the result being more harmful to you than to them. If the mother cited above would not have taken charge of her need for recognition and appreciation, she would have left it up to her daughter, guests or other family members. If she received appreciation, her need would be met. That is, if she believed the feedback and that she was deserving of appreciation.

Children fail to give their parents recognition that is due them, not because they do not feel it; instead, it is more related to children getting into the excitement of the moment, getting their basic psychological needs met, and just being kids. These needs include being taken care of, recognized, appreciated, valued, affirmed, and celebrated. Children learn to be appreciative as these needs for them are met; it is an ongoing process. I know many adults who find it difficult to genuinely appreciate others and what they do.

The mother who gave the party had the choice of blaming others for a lack of compliments in spite of her being deserving of accolades. She knew that it was out of her control to force appreciation and that judging served to preoccupy her thoughts with blame. She chose to use the same mental energy to compliment herself and increase her self-esteem and integrity. When you blame another, you erode your own self-respect; you use excessive emotional energy while believing judgment will change his/her behavior.

On the contrary, the opposite is true. As you respect and love yourself, others have the opportunity to feel your respect, thereby, creating a more optimal climate for change and growth. Behavioral change blossoms in an atmosphere of respect, not judgment. Judgments affect children and yourself like hailstones affect budding flowers.

Since this chapter emphasizes the importance and benefit of reflection in the parent-child relationship, it is necessary to look at the parenting tool of reflection by itself.

### → Reflection: A Necessary Parenting Tool and Guide

Reflection is an isolated, independent, and internal thought process that does not require anyone or anything outside yourself. It is very personal and private in that you are the one who is thinking back from your parental perspective to when you were a child. You, the character, stays the same and the difference is the number of years from when you were the child to the age you are now.

As you think back, you remember being the child with everything that included being dependent and powerless or independent and powerful, feeling much or little responsibility, feeling cared for or on your own, feeling important or unimportant, feeling lovable or unlovable, feeling worthwhile or not worthwhile, feeling protected or scared, or feeling connected to your family or isolated.

You remember specific events and situations. At times, your memory is so vivid that it feels as though the situation happened yesterday. It is impossible to get that picture out of your head. You remember times from infancy, pre-school, middle childhood, and adolescence.

Your present vantage point includes much more maturity and wisdom to understand your childhood position in a way that you could not have understood it as a child.

Your thoughts and awareness from reflecting on your childhood are valuable tools for relating to your children. You have been there and know the territory. The payoff from your contemplation about an earlier period of your life grants you the opportunity to heighten your understanding and sensitivity while clarifying and redefining. Clarifying means identifying what you experienced that was nurturing or destructive. Redefining means deciding how you want to parent your children in a different way than you were parented.

Reflection is a necessary and powerful parenting tool in your parent tool kit. It is a way of paying close attention just as you do in so many other areas of your life. It is watching the fuel gauge on your car gas tank, watching the deadline for paying your taxes, and paying your rent or mortgage. You know the disaster that could occur if you never entered the checks you wrote or balanced your checking account. Parenting, like your finances, takes constant monitoring.

## → Remember . . .

- You were once a child with the same needs, desires, wishes, dreams, and wants as your children.

- What you resolve from your childhood, as painful as it might be, eventually means psychological freedom for you.

- Children are powerless and dependent on adults.

- Your parents, unknowingly and unintentionally, took out their frustrations and unmet needs on you.

- Unless you know about your unmet needs and frustrations, you will take them out on your children.

- What you are conscious of is more in your control than what is subconscious for you; both effect your feelings and behaviors.

- It is never too late to make your childhood dreams come true.

- You are the only person to rewrite your life script.

- Reflection, a process of thinking and remembering, can help you to know where you are with yourself and your children.

**Chapter 2 Overview**

## Parents Are Very Important People

- Parents Are Very Important People
- The Role and Function: Big Shoes To Fill
- Many Roles Within the Main Role
- Your Major Training is On-The-Job
- Describe Rather Than Judge
- You Can Rely on Three Resources
- Impact vs Intent
- Kids' Logic vs Adults' Logic
- You Continue to Grow-Up as Your Kids Grow-Up
- What You as Parents Cannot Control
- What You as Parents Can Control
- For Your Journal
- Remember . . .

# 2

# Parents Are Very Important People

## Points to Ponder

- Your change from adult-child to parent is one of the profound times in your life.

- You have difficult, yet significant roles to live.

- You are so important that when you die, you cannot be replaced.

- Your parenting errors and mistakes are often erroneously interpreted as a diminishment of the job when just the opposite is true. A critical job means mistakes, errors and omissions: all opportunities for learning and growth.

- You spend little time thinking about your importance.

- Your parenting role and function mean *Big shoes to fill.*

- Your parenting role includes many responsibilities and demands that, at times, overshadow your other role: being an individual.

- Your belief in your importance and significance takes much self-love, self-acceptance, and forgiveness: a process that occurs in your thinking, not your feelings.

- Your parenting role includes many sub-roles— many hats to wear.

- Your major parenting training is on-the-job. Your level of preparation is not related to the significance of the role or your love for your children. All are separate issues.

- You experience less pain and allow for necessary changes to occur as you describe, not judge yourself and your role.

- Your primary parenting resource is having been a child who was parented which you may or may not want to remember.

- Your two other parenting resources are listening to your heart and intuition and sharing with other parents.

- Your remembering and believing in your importance, even when you do not feel important, keeps you mindful of your impact on your children.

- Your children, like you, may spend a lifetime freeing themselves of parental impact.

- You and your children have different viewpoints regarding the value of and the inherent tasks of parenting. As parents you may forget your childhood viewpoint of parents. In other words, there is a difference between kids' and adults' logic.

- You continue to grow-up as your children grow-up. Your level of maturity effects how you see yourself. It is never too late for you or your kids to believe in your importance.

- Your belief in your significance increases after your children are grown than when they are growing up. This is related to the fact that you and your children survived and/or grew-up.

- You as a parent control more than you do not control.

Explanations and examples about the preceding summary statements, based on workshop presentations, are discussed in the following text. As you read, remember to make any journal entries of thoughts and ideas that come to mind. Remember, your thoughts are important because they are yours; they are just as important as you are to your children.

## Parents Are Very Important People

The change from adult-child to parent is one of the most profound times in your life. Your other life transitions like entering public school, adolescence, high school or college, starting a career, or getting married do not include the same degree of responsibilities. The difference is you are the big person who is responsible for a little person. The transformation for you is so profound that the pictures in your head that you created about parenting slowly begin to change as do the answers that you were so sure about. There is no way to imagine the role until you are in the role.

You find yourself in difficult, yet significant roles to live. When your child is born, and throughout his/her growing years, you realize how unprepared you are for parenting and that there is no turning back. It is too late to change your mind now. Your child is here and is dependent on you. Your degree of significance increases with each year's growth and challenges. You are caught between knowing the miracle of your child's life and knowing the awesome responsibility of parenting.

You are the most important adult in your children's lives. This is true for both birth and adoptive parents. Other adults may love your children, yet no one is as connected to or invested in your child as you. You are so important that when you die, you cannot be replaced. A child who loses a parent spends her lifetime healing her loss. It is the greatest loss a child can experience. The thought is constantly with her wondering what her life might be like if her mother or father were alive. Adults who fill in as parents and caretakers, no matter how loving or responsive they might be, never replace birth parents.

Your feelings of inadequacy or fatigue which create mistakes, errors, and omissions never negate your importance. On the contrary, your errors are opportunities for learning and growth. The impact from this importance will be felt by your children long after they no longer live with you. For some, becoming a parent just happened, and for others it was a deliberate and planned choice. Either way, you are very important to your children.

Your children might be able to tell you about your importance directly or only during a crisis. It seems that crises prompt them to say what is felt that is hard to say during routine daily living. Nevertheless, with or without their feedback, the fact remains the same: **Parents are very important people.**

At school and in my private practice as I listen to children's experiences, I am constantly reminded of a parent's importance. Children in school often spend days thinking about a parent's well-being if they are ill, or are having job-related problems, or are on overload with their own adult issues. I hear the child who is worried after hearing her father was just diagnosed with lymphatic cancer. I hear the child who cannot concentrate because his mother and father are constantly fighting. I hear the child who cannot stop thinking about her mother's work conflicts, the child wanting to call her mother daily to make sure she still has a job.

The message from children to me is, "My mom and dad are very important people." Clearly, your children recognize your importance. How often do you think about your importance?

Chances are this question gets sidelined by others: What can I make for dinner? Where can I find the time to prepare for my important meeting tomorrow? How long will my mother be sick and need my help? How can I stretch the paycheck more? Will my car tires last through the winter?

As I listen to parents, I hear at a deeper level, the question, "How can I believe in my importance when much of the time I feel inadequate to do the job?" I challenge you, as you read about the following aspects of your parenting job that are overlooked, to see the difference between your significance and how you feel about your role. In a way, it is like asking a fish to describe water. You are too close to you and your children to see the greater picture.

## The Role and Function: Big Shoes to Fill

Your role as a parent and how you function in the role are not the same. The role alone has certain qualities, characteristics, and expectations assigned to it, such as authority, responsibility, power, and omnipotence. Additionally, the role has certain tasks of which the primary one is to care for, train, teach, and guide children to reach responsible adulthood in eighteen years.

What a huge task! It is so big that you never feel as though you have finished or completed the task. Do you ever say, at the end of a busy day, "I am fully satisfied today. I listened with my full attention every time my son spoke. I took time to think about all of my responses. I met all of my children's physical and emotional needs. I spent adequate time taking good care of myself."

Of course, that never happens. It is not like a nine-to-five job, with weekends off, vacation time, fringe benefits, and bonuses. It does not have regular evaluations that include understanding, support, constructive feedback, and suggestions that assist you in feeling more comfortable and competent in parenting. The job is twenty-four hours a day, seven days a week, three-hundred sixty-five days a year for a minimum of eighteen to twenty years and then some. The job is never done!

The role is big shoes to fill, ones that are much bigger than your feet. You realize just how big the shoes are as your children grow. Filling the shoes is your function or how you perform the tasks.

The role, with its immensity of responsibility and demands, obscures the fact that you are an individual with your own needs and unresolved issues from your childhood. Your function in the role is also obscured by the complexity of tasks inherent in the role. In other societal roles as president, chief executive officer, police, administrator, doctor, or teacher, how that person functions in the role is as paramount as the role itself.

Because children for many years are powerless and dependent, in parenting, much emphasis is given to the role alone. Children are reliant on parents to fill the big shoes even when they are unable to do so. Parents are expected to have all the answers and be the authority because that is the role. Children, then, are at the mercy of the adult no matter how the adult is functioning. This is amplified and costly when there is abuse or neglect.

For example, I am reminded of a verbal, intelligent, and precocious three-year-old whose teenage parent had a party one evening, a common occurrence. Alcohol and drugs flowed freely and by 3:00 a.m. everyone had blacked out. The son woke up then, and when he could not rouse anyone, he became extremely frightened and panicked. He pushed zero on the telephone; an alert telephone operator kept him talking until the number could be traced, and the police could be sent to his home. He was taken into temporary foster care until his parent received professional help and learned to function more responsibly.

All that he went through was a traumatic time for him. The impact of the trauma taught him first, to not trust adults and secondly, to believe he was the only one in control. Both of these effects led to his having bossy and controlling behaviors with his teachers and peers. He needed to stay alert and in charge in order to survive. It took him years to learn that he could count on adults to take care of him. The role of parenting is critical, no matter how parents are functioning. **Parents are very important people.** How much do you believe this? If your belief in this statement is minimal or shaky, it is no doubt related to how lines get blurred between role and function.

Three factors compound and confuse the complex lines between your parenting role and parenting function. The first is the numerous sub-roles within the major role. Next is the fact that your major and significant training in parenting is on-the-job. The third is recognizing the difference and effects between describing and judging both the role and function. Each of these reasons are explained further.

## Many Roles Within the Main Role

Have you thought about the number of sub-roles parenting encompasses? No other job is so diverse. In real life the role includes:

| | |
|---|---|
| accountant | guide |
| arbitrator | juggler |
| bookkeeper | launderer |
| bottle washer | mechanic |
| caregiver | mediator |
| cheerleader | mentor |
| coach | nurse |
| confidant | nurturer |
| consultant | organizational engineer |

cook            paramedic
counselor       police person
dietician        referee
fence-setter     taxi driver
friend          teacher
gate-keeper

You have not received formal or adequate training to perform all of these sub-roles; however, you are called on to function in these capacities from time to time. If you are a trained accountant, you feel more adept handling financial records and payments for medical visits, school expenses such as tuition, lunches, field trips, dues for girl and boy scouts or 4-H memberships, dance, piano, or horse riding lessons. If you are a trained paramedic, your skills and competence are evident when there are physical injuries. At the other jobs, you do the best you can with the experience you have.

For one day, keep track of the varied tasks you perform. Jot them down in your journal. You truly are a jack-of-many-trades. You deserve much credit for the many hats you wear especially when you acknowledge that your major training is on-the-job.

## Your Major Training is On-The-Job

You have no other job that is so demanding, never-ending, all-encompassing and full-time. No other job has so little instruction with the only substantial training being on-the-job. No other job carries so much blame or judgment if things do not turn out well. No other job has long-lasting impact coupled with good intentions, commitment, and love. No other job has the potential for what happened to you the first eighteen years of your life as an asset and liability.

Your imagining of the job bears no resemblance to being in the job. Your knowledge and confidence were only shaken by actually becoming a parent. Your children are incapable of understanding this truth as you were as a child. When you say in a moment of frustration, "Wait until you are a parent," the statement falls on deaf ears; the only benefit for you is ventilation and copying your mother or father. Your on-the-job training is equivalent to asking how comfortable you would feel booking a reservation on an airline after being told this is the pilot's first flight, and she has had no previous training vs. knowing this pilot has been flying for twenty-seven years without a crash. When you are told that this is her first flight, that she is intelligent, sensitive, learns quickly and will not repeat mistakes, that you can sit back and enjoy your flight, this fosters apprehension.

You expect professionals to have many field experiences before they are on their own. However, this is not the case for parents.

There is no other way to gain experience than to go through it yourself, learning and synthesizing your own observations, conclusions, successes, and mistakes that become your reality, beliefs, and wisdom. Before you became a parent and heard from parents what the job was like, you had no way of relating to that input because you did not have experience. You had your ideas about what it would be like for you that were very idealized. There was no way of knowing the connection between the immense responsibility of parenting and what it is like to function day-by-day as a parent. When you have children you *know* that connection.

Your first-born grants you your status of parenthood. You and your first-born have something in common that does not exist between you and your second or third-born. You lack experience being a parent and your first child lacks experience in being parented by an experienced parent. You have never been a parent before, even though you might have had much contact with children; it is different with your own children. Your first-born, who senses your inexperience, also makes the footsteps for other children who might follow.

You gain parenting experience with your first-born who truly is your guinea pig and experimental child. How else can you gain experience? Likewise, for your first child, you are his/her guinea pig and experimental parent. In other words, you both are green rather than seasoned. If you have more children, each has the chance of benefitting from your practice with your first-born as you also have the advantage of the training time received on-the-job. Your children's temperaments and personalities' make-up will vary, calling for some new approaches and techniques in your parenting skills, yet you have the basic understanding about what it is to parent.

Any other job has a training and trial period during which recognition is given to the fact that you are new and allowances are made for errors. There is no such leniency in your parenting career. It is not just practice; it is the real thing.

It is self-respecting, during high stress and conflictive times, (in response to the effects of your minimal training) to say to your first-born, "This is the first time I am the parent of a seven, twelve or sixteen-year-old, and with my greenness, this is where I am. I am sure you sense my unsureness. I am not sure right now what is best for me to say or do. I am sure that I love you very much and need some more time to learn about my most important job—parenting. I will let you know when I am feeling more decisive within myself. Thank you for being patient with me."

Your honesty and frankness models honesty and frankness, fostering respect, a wonderful way of acknowledging your inexperience and not getting it confused with love. Your love for your child and your child's love for you are separate issues from your being inexperienced in the art of parenting, and from your child's having a parent who is being trained with each interaction and experience.

Knowing the difference between describing and judging is the third reason that lines get fuzzy between role and function and also aids in making the distinction between love and inexperience.

## Describe Rather Than Judge

Your vocabulary is saturated with judgment words: good-bad, positive-negative, right-wrong, smart-dumb, forgivable-unforgivable, comfortable-miserable, reasonable-unreasonable, appropriate-inappropriate, and sensitive-insensitive. Unfortunately, you give these labels to yourself when you make a mistake, fail to meet expectations that might be unreasonable from the beginning, need an indirect way to invite pity, support, and attention, or when you need to provide an outlet for ventilation and expression of intense feelings.

You use these labels when you forget that your preparation for parenting has no relationship to your significance to your children. In addition, there is a difference between an expectation that is unreasonable and saying that you or your child are unreasonable people.

Judgments for the giver and receiver victimize, diminish, create feelings of powerlessness, fear, frustration, misery, inner turmoil, and deplete physical and emotional energies. These are high costs when your energies are already taxed to the limit and what you do (as the most important adults in your children's world) has the chance of being copied by them.

The respectful and peace-enhancing option is to describe yourself, your child, and the incident or situation. If you value and know that much of the time you are patient and listen intently to your son when he needs to be heard, and if he catches you at a time when you have fourteen things on your mind, his request might be the breaking one. An understandable and common response might be, "Can't you see I'm at the max; you are putting me over the edge!" The implied judgment is that your son's request was unreasonable and that he was insensitive to you and your overload.

Your frustration level, not your son's request, put you over the edge. After your frustration is expressed by screaming at your son, the edge is taken off, and you see that your reaction was harsh.

Rather than judging, you say to yourself, "I usually am patient and responsive to my son. He is lucky to have me as his mother. I do have my limits and today is one of those times. My energy level is low, and I have more than my share of requests and demands. I reached my limits before the potatoes were burning, the telephone was ringing, and the baby got sick; Jimmy's request tipped the scales. I want to pay closer attention to my energy level. He does not deserve the projection of my fatigue. I will share that with him."

Your feelings presented in this way can teach Jimmy to learn to sense when you are on overload, which will modify the timing for his requests if it is not an emergency or life-threatening situation. When you choose to let go of judgment, and use describing instead, you create tranquility and acceptance while you are teaching him, or yourself, or both sensitivity to your mood.

If you choose to think in this peace-enhancing monologue, you keep your focus on each situation rather than generalizing, "I can't do anything right," or "I am a horrible mother for snapping at my son." Self-acceptance, the opposite of judgment, is modeled and fostered. As you are skilled at describing and not judging your self, you do the same for your children. Your child would rather hear "I can see that you do not have very much energy today" than "You are a lazy slob."

## You Can Rely on Three Resources

Your first and best resource is your childhood, knowing that you have created ways to learn, enjoy, and survive. The main difference between you and your child is twenty or thirty years, more bumps and bruises, more wisdom, less energy and optimism, more reality-testing behaviors, more joys and regrets, dreams to fulfill, and time passing rapidly. You have journeyed through your childhood, and your children are now in their childhood. The setting and times were different for you, yet childhood is childhood. When you have been to the same city that a friend has visited, you feel a bond with each other from your similar experiences, even though you each saw different streets and sights.

To capitalize on your childhood, use you or your child's birthday as a point to remember when you were the same age as your child is now. What was it like? How did you feel? What was important to you? Use this awareness to connect with your child, not manipulate. For example, "I didn't have a room of my own when I was a kid, so you should appreciate what you have." Your deprivation and your child's abundance are two separate issues. Don't confuse them. Be honest with how you wanted a room of your own and that you are able to give your daughter her own room.

Secondly, listen carefully to your heart, intuition and common sense. Over and over, I ask parents, "What was your first hunch?" Frequently, if they would have followed it, stress and conflict would have decreased. Believing in your importance gives you permission to listen to your heart. Important people have authority that comes from their hearts and common sense. Make sure that you do not overlook you.

Your last resource is talking and sharing with other parents to remind you that you are not alone with your questions, concerns, joys, and fears. You know how good it feels to hear that another person went through the same experience you had and survived. You make a connection by knowing that you have had similar experiences.

The following accounts from the lives of Sarajean and Martin illustrate how you as parents are very important people.

### Sarajean

I remember our school nurse telling me that Sarajean, age seven, came to her office five times before one o'clock. The symptoms changed hourly from a scratch on her arm to a stomachache to a headache to a blister on her heel that could hardly be seen. It became clear that her aches were more psychological than physical.

By listening carefully to her, I heard fear and panic. Since she was convinced that her feelings were valid and she needed to talk about what was churning inside of her, the events of the morning unfolded.

Mornings were chaotic and tense at her home. Her father had little tolerance for the three children's bickering, lollygagging, and just being kids. He needed to get to his work which was stressful enough. Sarajean was able to get herself ready while her one- and three-year-old brothers needed much care and supervision. All this taxed the time, energy, tolerance, and patience of her mom and dad who needed to be at work on time.

This morning her mother had overslept, having been up four times during the night with one-year-old Ryan. Three-year-old Jeremy woke up with excessive energy, and while he was riding his big wheel in the living room, he knocked over the large, freshly watered, potted palm.

While the family sat down to eat breakfast, mother cleaned a layer of dirt from the rug. As she was putting the bucket and sponge away, Dad flew past her with his briefcase and morning paper yelling, "I will never be back." Going to the kitchen to assess the situation, she saw all three children crying, and Sarajean wiping up the glass of milk Jeremy spilled when he was fighting with her over the piece of toast that had the most sugar and cinnamon.

Sarajean was sure she had caused her father to leave and was equally sure he was not coming back. If only she had given Jeremy the piece of toast he wanted. She hurt so much and was so scared. The one way she knew how to express her feelings was to convert them into physical symptoms. Adult assistance was necessary to get to her underlying fear.

I knew she needed to talk with her father directly and allowed her to call him at work. I could not speak for her father. I could hear and understand her distress. I could help her take ownership for her part of the morning scenario.

Fortunately for both of us, he answered her call. Before saying hello and between sobs she said, "Daddy, please come home tonight. I promise to not fight with Jeremy at breakfast. It is all my fault. I am sorry. Are you O.K.? Please come home tonight."

As I talked to him briefly, I told him he was the most important male in her life. The frustration he felt at breakfast equalled the distress his daughter was feeling at school. He needed to acknowledge and accept his humanness, forgive himself, and reassure his daughter he still cared and would not abandon her.

The incident had more to do with frustration, yet love was questioned. Parents and children alike frequently confuse the two. Had he been someone else who was at the end of his rope, the impact would not have been so great. The greater the importance of the person you love (or fear), the greater the impact.

## Martin

Martin moved to a neighboring state in August the day after he celebrated his eighth birthday. He hated to leave his friends in the familiar neighborhood.

It was most difficult leaving Jason whom he had known since birth. They were born in the same hospital just six hours apart, lived on the same block, and were in the same classes since preschool. They were like brothers.

Also Martin did not know when he would see his father again. Family life was relatively stable until eleven months ago when his father had a psychotic break-down and the prognosis for recovery looked bleak. At best, rehabilitation would take considerable treatment and time. Job stress and financial worries, aggravated by unresolved historical trauma, precipitated his hospitalization.

Next mother decided to moved to be near her family for support and help with child-care. She needed time and assistance while she adjusted to becoming the only emotional and financial provider for the family.

Martin's mother enrolled him in third grade and his sister in first grade. In his new school Martin was assigned to the only male teacher, Mr. Riley. Martin liked Mr. Riley instantly even though he had never had a male teacher.

Martin called Jason that evening and both shared how they missed each other and compared notes of their first day in third grade.

Jason momentarily thought about wanting to share his excitement about his new school with his father and remembered that was not possible. Why had this happened to his father?

However, he knew he would enjoy the two classroom computers and the bunny who roamed freely in the room. He already had some names in mind for the contest to name the classroom mascot. He felt included when his classmates selected his entry of Peepers as the bunny's name.

Then two weeks before parent-teacher conference time in November, Martin was involved in numerous playground fights with students from other classes. This behavior soon expanded to peers in his classroom. When he was reprimanded for his part in the fighting, he consistently would view the situation as being unfair.

His mother was exhausted from the frequent calls from the school principal and the constant fighting with his sister. Martin refused to cooperate with peers or adults, and every interaction became a battleground.

My hunch was that he was feeling the effects of the loss of his father's presence and availability to Martin and his family. By November it had been almost a year since his father's hospitalization, and his absence was a painful reality. How could he mourn the loss of someone who was still alive and had been so present until a year ago? He could not, so he released his pent-up emotions by fighting.

Toward the end of the school year, he was able to reluctantly acknowledge his loss and heightened distress. How does a child believe something that is so unfair, has nothing to do with him yet has such an extensive impact? How can he deal with the feelings of rejection and alienation?

For many years Martin will need prudent guidance from significant adults to understand his pain and to guide him to not allow his pain to invite rejection and alienation from others. Only to the degree that he can resolve what was out of his control and so painful can he find a peaceful sense of himself. What a challenge for a child who deserves a lighter load! Life is unkind at times.

While both of these situations show what children and parents experience in daily life while pointing out the parents' significance, there are two other distinctions that relate indirectly to your parenting role and function. The first one is understanding the difference between intent and impact. The second is understanding the difference between kid and adult logic.

## Impact vs. Intent

In your parent-child relationship there are two terms that are frequently confused. Understanding these two terms, impact and intent, and the difference between them, clarifies some aspects of the interpersonal process that enhance or erode peacefulness and self-respect.

How many times have you said or heard, "I didn't know you took it that way; I didn't mean it like that; You heard me wrong; I thought I said . . .; What I meant to say (or do) was . . . ; I can see I hurt you; I never intended any harm."

While intent is what you expect and want (or do not expect) to happen, impact is what does happen. Impact is the feelings and messages your child receives from his/her vantage point of the situation which includes what you parents say and do. The younger the child, the more tendency there is for the child to take the impact of the situation as a statement about him/her which gets internalized and included in the child's beliefs about him/herself.

Impact for your child is felt when you are not thinking about how what you say or do affects your child. Impact is also felt by your child when her needs and your needs conflict at the same time. For instance, if a father is dealing with problems at work and he is afraid of losing his job, the stress he feels will preoccupy his time and attention. His daughter's needs for his time and attention will go unmet.

It does not mean that the important adults intentionally want to hurt children in any way by not giving them the assistance they deserve. Adults are human and can be overpowered by their own feelings especially during stressful or frightening times. Sometimes the situation is for an overwhelming concern for the child's safety. For example, when a child is found after being lost in a department store, the parents' feelings of fear and relief overshadow the need to think how frightened the child is also. What the child feels gets buried and may not surface until as a parent he finds himself in a similar situation with his child.

In lost-child scenes, I observe parents who are scared to death, converting their fear to rage and royally scolding the child. In this situation, the message to the child is "I am furious and you did something bad." How scared the parent is, the primary feeling, never gets communicated. The child believes he caused the rage and is a bad person. What the child is feeling gets totally lost and overlooked. Impact is powerful and long-lasting.

Unless adults are out-of-control with their emotions and choose to be vindictive or punishing, what primarily happens between parent and child is much more related to interpersonal impact than intent. The second difference occurs between kids' and adults' logic.

## Kids' Logic vs. Adults' Logic

Young children have not yet learned to think in abstract ways, so they hear what parents say in a literal way and then take what they hear to heart. Children personalize parents' comments and do not realize parents are saying how they are feeling inside them.

Adult logic is based on years of experience and trial-and error-learning; it is called maturity. Adult logic is thinking that makes sense to you just as kid logic makes sense to your children. Adult logic is the conclusion(s) drawn from your thinking that serves as the basis for your feelings and your behavior. The difference between kid and adult logic is exemplified in the following account of a little boy named Roger.

## Roger

Roger was two-years old when his parents separated after a tumultuous marriage. He does not remember a time when he lived with both of his parents. He enjoys looking at family pictures before the separation and divorce and will often ask questions.

Both parents remarried and established stable relationships when Roger was almost four. Since he was in joint-custody and his parents lived two miles apart, he adjusted comfortably to the household routines. His parents had grown within themselves and in their new relationships, had become respectful of each other, and could talk without fighting about Roger's needs and well-being.

In first grade, Roger had the opportunity with his advanced reading and writing skills to publish a classroom book. Students were encouraged to select a topic, write the text and illustrate the book. His teacher did the typing and publishing. He named his book, *My Wish.*

On each page were the following lines, each with an accompanying picture. *I am Roger. When I was a babee I lived with my mom and dad. They had fites. My dad got his hus. It has a red dor. He lives with Linda. I like Linda. My mom lives with Gary. He is nice. My mom and dad do not fite now. I want all of us to live in a big hus. We can hav fon.*

As Roger was growing up, his parents each gained more control over their lives, thereby, projecting less onto each other and decreasing the fighting between them. The change was fortunate for them and unfortunate for Roger and his need to have both parents loving each other and living in the same house. Fortunately, for Roger he slowly understood that his parents had changed too much to live together; however, the change allowed them to respect each other and love Roger. For each of them and Roger, their changes of increased self-respect and peacefulness, modeled respect and peacefulness.

Gaining more control over your lives and projecting less on each other are the same as you as parents continuing to grow up with your children. You continue to chart your seas while you guide your children. No wonder the seas feel rough at times. That is a big job!

## You Continue to Grow Up as Your Kids Grow-Up

Your growth does not stop when you become adults. You continue to go through your developmental stages as do your children. Your life span is quite short when you consider all, especially your thinking, that potentially can impact and influence your growth. You learn in the same way that your children learn. You observe and watch other people, think and rehearse the action in your mind, act the behavior, practice the behavior, and expand the repertoire of behaviors into other actions and learning. In other words, learning starts with your thinking, changes to doing by learning, and then to learning by doing.

Each day both you and your children learn new information, skills, and ideas. Use your journal as a way of keeping track of your new learning even though it might seem easier for you to keep track of your children's new learning. Yet, you as a VIP (Very Important Person) need to follow your growth too. It takes a long time to become grown-up with all the respect and peacefulness you deserve, and all parents are on that same road, perhaps at different points. There are some events (See list at the end of this chapter.) that are not in your control and many happenings that are in your control. Your continued learning includes becoming aware of what you do and do not control. What you have most control over is your thinking.

It is easy to believe that you have less control than you do, resulting in feelings of powerlessness, eroding your self-respect, and depleting your physical and emotional energies. Assessing these beliefs periodically is a source of emotional energy and personal respect.

My postscript to you on this critical topic, Parents Are Very Important People, is sharing a list of what you do and do not control.

→ **What You as a Parent Cannot Control**

- Choosing your parents, grandparents or great-grandparents.

- Your parents' unresolved issues from their childhoods.

- Your gender and genetic endowment.

- What your parents did or did not give you.

- The choices your parents made and make.

- Circumstances in your historic family.

- The number and gender of your siblings.

- Your parents' level of self-esteem, control, and discipline.

- Your parents' communication style, life philosophy, morals, religious beliefs, political standings, cohorts, and the reputations they developed for themselves.

- Social and political changes in your world.

- How other parents parent their children.

- The weather and taxes.

- How others perceive you as a person and parent.

- The gifts and emotional baggage your co-parent brings to your relationship and parenting.

- The gender and genetic endowment of your children.

- What others listen to, understand, or agree with what you say.

- How your children think.

- Your children's choice of friends.

- Whom your children marry.

- Your grandchildren's genetic endowment.

→ **What You as a Parent Can Control**

- How much control you now give your parents to control or define you.

- If or how much you choose to accept and love your parents as human beings.

- The degree to which you choose to forgive your parents for their neediness, mistakes, errors, and humanness.

- Changing rather than repeating your history.

- Accepting your gender and genetic endowment.

- The creation of your gender identity.

- Loving yourself.

- The degree of significance you give to your parenting role.

- How much you diminish and berate yourself.

- The time you allow to learn parenting skills.

- Giving yourself credits for jobs well done.

- Taking good care of yourself.

- Knowing your birthright entitles you to believe you are wonderful, marvelous, lovely, lovable, and valuable.

- Your thinking and beliefs which create your feelings and create your behavior.

- Learning from your mistakes.

- Your reactions to your children.

- How accepting you are of your children's mistakes.

- Loving your children.

- Taking charge of yourself.

- Believing you project how you feel onto others; when you look at them, you are looking in a mirror, not through a clear glass.

- What you choose to resolve from your childhood so as not to displace it onto your children.

- Your communication style.

- The degree of respect and openness you feel for yourself and your children.

- Being clear about what you want to say before you speak.

- Knowing that being a parent is perpetuation of the human race.

- Believing when your children are adults you will say parenting certainly was a learning experience; if you had a second chance there are many things you would do very differently. One thing is certain: you loved them and did the best you could do.

- Believing whatever else your children need to finish growing up, they will find the resources to do so.

→ **For Your Journal**

Now create your own lists in your journal. Be very specific and personal. Review your lists from time to time. As you take more control of your life, you let go of other people or events that are not in your control. In your control is noting the times when you are aware of your importance to your children.

→ **Remember . . .**

- You will never be the same since becoming a parent; it is not good or bad—it is.

- Your own children provide you with an experience that you cannot obtain in any other way.

- It is amazing how your understanding of your parents increases when you become a parent.

- There is never enough time to think about your parenting role and responsibilities; you are too busy doing the job.

- You are wonderful and important to your children even when you do not feel the same way.

- Be careful to not confuse feelings of frustration with feelings of love. They are very separate.

- Give yourself credit for all you do.

- You will be a parenting genius when your kids are all grown.

- Take charge of what you can control and let go of the rest. That is more than enough for you to handle.

**Chapter 3 Overview**

**Building And Maintaining Trust**

- **Trust: A Determining Building Block in the Child-Parent Relationship**
- **What is Trust?**
- **Learning to Trust is a Gradual Process**
- **Trust and Doubt are Opposites**
- **How Trust Develops**
- **The Degree to Which You Trust Yourself is the Degree to Which You are Trusting of Your Children**
- **As Children Sense Your Belief in Their Trustworthiness, They Start to Behave in Trustworthy Ways**
- **The Cart Before the Horse?**
- **Breaking Trust**
- **For Your Journal**
- **Remember . . .**

# 3

# Building and Maintaining Trust

## Trust:

- develops in the intrapersonal and interpersonal process of living and loving and is a learned attitude. It is a determining building block in your relationship with your children.

- is letting go and allowing your kids to do for themselves what they are capable of doing: a process that evolves slowly and needs frequent reassessing.

- begins within you and is synonymous with "believing in."

- is a feeling that develops within you and between you and another person that is felt more often than it is verbalized.

- in yourself is knowing what you think, believe, and want; it is not what others, especially historical or current authority figures, think, or want.

- and doubt are opposites. Trust creates kindness, risking, encouragement, patience, hope, forgiveness, acceptance, peace, warmth, openness, respect, and closeness and brings out the best in you; doubt creates feelings of fear, diminishment, anxiety, depression, rage, powerlessness, vindictiveness, suspiciousness, and distance and brings out the worst in you and your children.

- in yourself enhances your joy and self-fulfillment and invites others to perceive you as being credible and trustworthy.

- is initially based on beliefs, not accomplishments and performance. Belief precedes performance and achievement. Then performance and accomplishments confirm and reinforce the initial belief. This is true within you and between you and your child.

- in your children relates directly with your trust in yourself. In other words, the degree to which you trust your children, that is, believe they are trustworthy even though their behavior at a given time is the opposite, is directly related to your level of self-trust.

- is a very important factor in self-esteem and self-respect.

- develops in children as they sense significant adults believe in their capability to be trustworthy.

- involves teaching with your actions and words. If your actions and words are discrepant, the message your children believe is from your behavior.

- involves knowing the myth that puts the cart before the horse: "Show me you are trustworthy and I will trust you."

- takes much longer to build than to tear down. One angry and out-of-control interaction destroys months and years of kindness. Be gentle . . . .

### Trust: A Determining Building Block in the Child-Parent Relationship

As parents, most of you agree about the importance of trust in the parent-child relationship, yet generally you are unaware of the processes of building and maintaining trust which become more complicated as your children grow. Trust is a determining building block in your relationship with your children. To trust is to gradually let go of your children, allowing them to learn to shift from dependency and reliance on you, to dependency and reliance on themselves. In theory, this is what all parents want.

In practice, it is a different story since your needs of dependency and independency color your perceptions, getting in the way of how you view your children. In other words, how much you have learned to rely on yourself and not on historical or current authority figures, such as parents, supervisors, and community leaders, affects your level of self-trust and independence.

Your child has all he/she needs to develop self-trust, and your task is to provide the interpersonal environment for trust to grow. Each interaction with you parents and other significant adults provides feedback to your child about his/her trustworthy capability. This feedback to your child is thwarted in situations where you have a need for your child to behave in certain ways for your benefit, to make you feel good, rather than for your child's well-being. Your need, rather than your child's need is primary.

I remember a session with an intelligent, capable, and reasonable fifteen-year-old boy who told me that his father always wanted him to "do everything his (father's) way." The son was insightful enough to know that his father's need to be so controlling came from his self-doubt, not his self-trust. "Everything" included tying his shoes, hosing the driveway, slicing bread, choosing his friends, organizing his school work, washing the car, or doing his laundry.

I asked the son what happened if he agreed to do a task and he did it his way. He replied that he always did the task the way his father wanted it done, so his father would not get mad. It was easier for the son to let his father be in control than to tolerate his father's anger. "Doing it his father's way" was for his father's need. Dependency on his father kept his father from getting angry and delayed the son's learning to trust himself. There are many different ways of doing tasks.

The father's behavior pattern started when he was a child who did not have any input into how he wanted to respond to his father. The choice was to do tasks the way his father wanted them done or receive his father's rage. Each choice is costly for a child and creates dependency and fear. Each choice supports the power of history repeating, not changing. Neither is trust-enhancing.

## What is Trust?

Trust is a feeling that develops within you (intrapersonal) and between you and another person (interpersonal) that is felt more often than it is verbalized. You know the calm, ease, peace, and sense of freedom that you feel when you are trusting yourself. In like manner, you know whom you trust and for what reasons, yet you may never openly share the reasons. In both instances you know the preciousness when trust is there. In contrast, you know the uneasiness when trust is absent within you and between you and others.

Trust, to your children, says you can count on me to keep your best interest in mind, to not be hurtful, to accept your weaknesses and highlight your strengths, to recognize you, to not pull any surprises except pleasant ones, to listen to you, to think the best, to keep your confidence, and if in doubt, to always err on the gentle side.

Trust in yourself is relying on your best judgment. It is claiming or reclaiming your birthright of peacefulness, fulfillment, and being yourself; it is not running your thoughts through another's head, thinking you need to defer to his/her wishes or needs; it is not bypassing yourself.

It is knowing what you believe. It is not what others, especially historical authority figures, believe. If your belief is unclear, it is allowing yourself time to think and decide what you want. As your children grow, they want (with your permission) to know what they believe.

This is a difficult shift for children to make, since for so many years they needed to depend on you and listen to what you wanted and felt was best for them. The counterpart, and just as difficult for you as parents, is to let go graciously, slowly, and gently while believing in your children's capability to master personal and life-skills. You often have difficulty letting go because you do not understand the difference between overpowering and having influence. Your nonexistent parenting class excluded this topic.

In your teacher and mentor role, you obviously have influence on your children. Influence is incorporating into your life what you have learned by watching someone's behavior or listening to what she says, selecting the parts that you want to make your own. The key is translating and incorporating whatever you choose to learn from someone else into your beliefs and attitudes, making it yours, and then knowing (trusting) how to make it work best for you.

Overpowering occurs when parents are so unsure of themselves that they insist on their children supporting and validating them. The parents' needs overpower the child, and the child does not have the opportunities to think for him/herself and practice behaviors that develop self-trust.

Letting go also includes knowing that your children will not behave in the same manner as you. Do you behave and respond in exactly the same way as your parents? No, yet you do have some behaviors that are similar to your parents. You have been influenced by them and are yourself. You are not a clone of your parents, and your children are not a clone of you. Expecting them to be exactly like you creates frustration, making trust between you impossible. The development of trust, like letting go, is a gradual process.

## Learning to Trust is a Gradual Process

Learning to trust is a gradual process that continues for a lifetime. Trust is experienced by infants at birth when they sense that significant adults can be counted on to give care that satisfies their needs for food, warmth, elimination, and protection. Trust is felt and learned as these needs are met.

For most parents, you find it easier to feel trusting of yourself when your children are young and dependent. Before your child masters skills, you know that he/she has the capability to do so. Your trust in your child increases as you observe his/her readiness to turn over, hold a bottle and spoon, jump, and ride a bicycle. Your excitement about your child's mastery of milestones such as rolling over, reaching for objects, crawling, walking, feeding and dressing himself, talking, and toileting allows you to give him/her room to gain more independence.

The room you give, along with encouragement, provides the practice time your child needs to become more skilled at specific tasks. Each new task that your child masters increases his/her independence and corresponding level of self-trust. You feel elated that your child is gaining independent skills and you share your elation with grandparents and friends who can cherish your joy. At times you may take credit that really goes to your child—her intelligence, readiness, interest, muscle development, and determination. You assist your child and your child does the growing. You can take credit for your assistance, and the rest of the credit goes to your child.

Children's physical needs, as opposed to emotional needs, are more clearly defined, helping you to respond confidently. Shelter, nutritional, and safety needs are more obvious than needs of esteem, trust and individualization, yet the process of trust is the same for both.

Your comfort zone with responding to and caring for them in early years is sharply contrasted as they reach the teen years when self-trust is their all-encompassing developmental task. Their individuation and separation summon physical and emotional distance which can be threatening, telling you that you are not needed as much as in the earlier years. If and how you personalize (believe children are saying more about you than themselves) their developmental tasks, you allow their self-trust to threaten and erode your self-trust. Vicious power struggles emerge with power, control, manipulation, and vindictiveness being primary; trust gets lost.

Your sense of yourself does not come from your children; it comes from within you. If you ever need self-trust, it is now. You can never believe too much in the wonderful, marvelous and lovely person—you. Believing in your weaknesses is doubt, not trust.

## Trust and Doubt Are Opposites

Trust and doubt are opposites and cannot exist together at the same time. Trust creates feelings of hope, tranquility, love, and powerfulness, while doubt creates feelings of fear, powerlessness, vindictiveness, and suspicion. Trust is believing that if the worst does happen, you will find a way to respond and even learn an important lesson. Doubt is knowing that the worst will happen and that you will not recover.

Trust says, "I believe in myself and you," and doubt says, "I do not believe in myself and you." Trust is optimistic; doubt is pessimistic. Trust is proactive knowing what you think; conversely, doubt is reactive countering and defending yourself against what someone else thinks and says. Trust brings out the best in you. Doubt brings out the worst in you.

Trust enhances your sense of joy and self-fulfillment inviting others to view you as happy, genuine, and trustworthy. Doubt destroys your energy and vitality, inviting others to see you as a defeated individual, shrouded in gloom. Doubt is wearing a tee shirt that says, "Don't trust me. I don't trust myself."

My experience with children is that when they feel trusted, their responses are sensitive, cooperative, caring, warm, tender, kind, empathic, and affectionate. Opposite responses come from not feeling trusted.

## How Trust Develops

Trust is a learned trait that is cultivated interpersonally. It develops within you and between you and others and vice versa. The circular formation of individual trust is contingent on verbal and non-verbal messages such as, "You can count on me to keep your well-being and best interest in mind; I am trustworthy; I believe in you; I can see your wonderful potential and capability; I will not ridicule or punish you; I know that all you attempt to do and do is an opportunity to grow; I accept and do not judge you; I know that you can do it and will succeed; With your intelligence, dedication, and hard work, it is impossible for you to fail."

Trust is initially based on beliefs, not accomplishments and performance. Belief precedes performance and achievement; then performance and accomplishments confirm and reinforce the initial belief. In other words, before you do something, you think or believe that you can. As you accomplish what you thought you could, you believe and know that you can. After repeated practice, the task is commonplace, and you do not even question your competency.

Do you remember when you learned to drive a car? You knew that you wanted to and could learn how to drive. At first, you observed other drivers and listened to your teacher's instructions. You were aware of each step from putting on your seat belt, adjusting your rear view mirror, reviewing the function of the gears, seeing what was close to you, putting the key in the ignition, and so on. With more practice, you did not have to stop and reflect on each step. It became a familiar pattern, and you now trust your ability to drive a car. You might even trust in your ability to drive safely, citing that you have never had an accident.

Your belief in your children's physical capability might be greater than your belief in their social, academic, or emotional capability. Did you question if your daughter would roll over, walk, jump, or talk? You believed it would happen. Do you question if your son will have the clear thinking and judgment to handle himself in a difficult situation? The latter takes longer to develop trust since those are the more challenging areas for adults to feel trusting of themselves.

You know people whose strong beliefs helped them to fight and survive illness, accidents, and other traumatic times even when the odds were against them. People like this, who believe in (trust) themselves are an inspiration and source of strength and encouragement to others.

There are no shortages of opportunities to develop trust in your children; every day common situations provide openings for trust-building. For instance, most parents teach their children the routine household job of setting the table for meals. You believe (trust) that your child can learn this task and soon do the job without prompting and cuing.

How many times has your child seen you put the plates, glasses, napkins, and silverware on the table? Of course, the times are too numerous to tally. It is a familiar occurrence. Your child has a general idea that those items go on the table and maybe has not observed the exact placement of the items. You may have a certain order of how you like the plate, glass, napkin, knife, fork, and spoon arranged. You learned that from your mother.

The first several times your son sets the table he might get all of the items on the table even though they are put in a different order. A reactive, short-sighted, or omnipotent comment, "You did it all wrong," would destroy trust while a proactive comment, "You got everything on the table, You are a wonderful helper, Thank you," would enhance trust. Time can be given at some future point to teach a different order of placement of the table settings. In between times, your child may observe you setting the table and may copy what you do. Children tune into details more when they have had experience with a given task.

What happens within you affects what happens between you and your child. Likewise, what happens between you and your child affects what happens within your child.

## The Degree to Which You Trust Yourself is the Degree to Which You Are Trusting of Your Child

Trust and trusting begin within you and developed for you when you were a child. When you enter parenthood, your need for self-trust is intensified since your child's development of trust is contingent on you. You cannot bypass yourself. Your children sense when there is a difference between what you say to them and how you feel. Telling them not to be so critical and your criticizing them and others, much of the time, send a double message. The messages, "Of course, you can sleep in your bed all night, I know you can learn to color in the lines, and I know you will learn your multiplication tables," are cancelled if you feel your own self-doubt.

Your child is sensitive to you, and when a discrepancy exists between your verbal and behavioral message, the message your child receives and believes is what goes on inside of you. In other words, your child senses your fear and doubt even though your words may say the opposite. This is awesome, scary, powerful, and true. Your children are unable to do as you say when your behavior is the opposite. As stated in earlier chapters, that is the power, impact, and challenge of parental modeling. Remember, parents are very important people.

If this were not true, kids would listen to what parents say, and self-defeating behaviors would be non-existent. I never hear a father tell his daughter to not study and fail her final math exam, or a mother tell her son to be careless and have an accident, or a father tell his daughter to torment her little brother and act up in school, or other messages to destroy others' belongings, be hurtful to people, or be inconsiderate of adults.

You are fortunate if you grew up with adults who, from their self-trusting position, were able to believe in you even before you developed trustworthy behaviors. Conversely, if you grew up with parents who were fearful, critical, judgmental or suspicious, it could be difficult for you to be trusting of your children even though you are trustworthy. If not, as an adult, you have the responsibility of believing more in you. All this emphasizes is that trust is learned—a joy and challenge for you of what you teach. Think how despairing it would be if trust were genetic? Either you would have it or you would not, and there would be nothing you could do about it. Trust is taught by parents who believe in themselves.

### As Children Sense Your Belief in Their Trustworthiness, They Start to Behave in Trustworthy Ways

By this time you know the dilemma of teaching what you have not mastered yourself. Can you teach how to formulate and solve an algebra problem when you have had no instruction? How would you begin to learn to drive a car if you never rode in one or took a driver's education class?

I meet with countless parents who know they want their children to trust themselves and, in a most articulate way, share how Susie is failing two courses because they are sure that she does not think that she is smart and can do the work. All she has to do is know that she can do it.

I kindly respond with, "I wish, too, it were that simple. Unfortunately, it is not." The critical missing part is in the answer to the question, "How much do you, mother or father, believe in you? Only you know the answer." Parents get tears in their eyes as they share their awareness of their lack of self-trust, yet know that they want so much for their children to have more self-trust.

Your belief in yourself gives your child permission to trust in him/herself. Your children sense if your attitude is skeptical (coming from your self-doubt) or is credible, (based on your self-trust).

As children feel trustworthy, their behavior is the same. You cannot put the cart before the horse.

## The Cart Before the Horse?

Steps in the process of building trust are as ordered as the horse being in front of the cart. Just as common as the statement, "All she has to do is know she can do it," is the parental reply, "I refuse to trust him until he proves he is worthy of my trust. He has to earn it. Even then, he will need to prove it over and over before I will believe. I can't count on him to do anything. I tell him to do a simple job like empty the trash. That's not too hard! Is it? I know he won't do it! I've taken so many things away from him, there isn't anything left. He doesn't care. There isn't any hope for him."

This father would be more honest and enhance his level of trust if he said, "I know I'm a hard-nosed Dad. My doubt is greater than my trust, and I won't let my son forget it. Why should I make it smooth for him? My dad was so pessimistic and mean; he put every roadblock in my way he could. I see now how he was persist-ent and creative. He out-maneuvered me, and I made it in spite of him. I never got encouragement, support, acceptance, warmth, and for sure, no respect. My son is no better than me."

To him I said, "I agree. You are both wonderful and creative males who have learned to deal with resistance and adversity and have no doubt devised ways of retaliating and inviting the same from each other. You deserve more than your father got from his father. I am impressed that you chose to risk talking to me and had the courage to open your heart about your son. Do you think your father ever sat in a counselor's office?"

This father's attitude of harshness, skepticism, and rejection reflected his childhood relationship with his father, guaranteeing to maintain mistrust rather than trust with his son. Mistrust invites mistrust and is perpetuated by the myth, "Show me that you are trustworthy and then I will trust you."

When trust is present between parent and child, it can be shat-tered more easily than it is built.

### Breaking Trust

Trust is destroyed quicker than it is built. Cutting, nasty, angry words, and interactions can destroy trust that has taken years to establish.

The paradox is that what is so strong and precious is also a guaranteed way of shattering and destroying a child's spirit. How can, what is so strong, be so fragile?

The example of Janet highlights how children hurt from untrue accusations and how their struggle to believe in themselves is an uphill battle.

### Janet

Janet fought back tears as she said the accusations from her mother were not true. "I don't do what she says I do, and if she doesn't stop, I might. How can I convince my own mother that she is wrong? It feels like a losing battle. I don't even want it to be a battle."

"I have always been a serious and honest student since kindergarten. I get good grades and always do my homework. I don't smoke and drink like a lot of kids I know. I hang around with good kids. I know I have good judgment. I have never given her any reason to doubt me. She won't even believe my friends or their parents. They tell her how responsible, honest, polite, and dependable I am. She says they are all covering for me. I can't convince her that I don't want to mess up my life. It's my life. I am so afraid that I will get so mad at her that I will do something stupid to get back at her, and I will have to live with the consequences. I couldn't live with myself if that happened. I hate the fix I am in."

Janet was in her mid-teens and had countered her mother's accusations for what seemed like forever. She needed someone who would believe in her. Her mother's lack of trust and suspicious attitude did not come from Janet's behavior. There was no reason for mother not to trust Janet. As you might suspect, her mother's lack of trust came from her mother's unresolved relationship with her mother whose suspicious attitude blocked trust from developing between them. False accusations hurt and destroy trust. Janet was the recipient of many generations of mistrust between mothers and daughters. History is powerful unless looked at and changed.

The following example of Crystal, with different circumstances than Janet, shows how children strive to prove their trustworthiness, how they persist, how they have not yet learned to draw the line between what is their issue and what is their parents' issue, and how quickly trust is crushed.

### Crystal

As the third of six daughters, Crystal had to find her own special way of being unique. Her oldest sister was tense and frequently irritable, her next sister was a book-worm, so since she was bubbly and energetic, she chose to be the "love" sister. She thrived on telling her mother and father she loved them and looked for ways that she could be supportive and helpful.

When Crystal was ten, child number seven, a son arrived to complete their busy household. Dad was elated to exit his minority status. He grew up with five sisters and often felt over-powered by the gender inequity. Crystal welcomed her brother and added caretaker to her role. She loved to hold and rock him in the antique rocking chair that belonged to her great-grandmother.

The love in Crystal's heart multiplied ten-fold; her elation prompted her to sometimes go overboard with her graciousness. Part of it was genuine while another part was compensatory to meet her needs. When she needed attention, she was helpful, and she hoped for acknowledgement of her kind deeds.

Sensing her mother's fatigue and severe post-partem depression, she helped more to lighten her mother's load. She was like a hawk watching for tasks to do.

Mother's exhaustion became chronic. Crystal remained vigilant with her help and assurances of her love. Given mother's physical and emotional state, she was unable to believe, yet alone respond to her young daughter's level of responsiveness. Mother remembered better times, and her rage and guilt clouded her thinking.

One day when Crystal was telling her mother how much she loved her, her mother snapped, "You don't love me. You hate me." The shock, dejection, and pain were indescribable. It was as though a part of Crystal died at that moment. She was unable to realize that her mother's reply was a statement of her mother's weakened condition which had nothing to do with Crystal. Yet Crystal's spirit was broken by seven words in seven seconds in an atmosphere of disbelief.

→ **For Your Journal**

Make a journal entry of the people (past and present) in your life who were/are trusting of you. Think about what it was/is about them that makes them trusting. Be specific about the behaviors you identify. For example, you might identify his sense of humor, her accepting and non-judgmental attitude, his welcoming invitations, her easy-going behaviors, and his ability to listen without interrupting.

Reflect on the behaviors and select the behaviors that were most helpful to you in developing self-trust. If you choose to copy those behaviors, allow ample time for practice. Practicing and practiced behaviors become commonplace and part of you. Reflect on and record the changes that enhance your self-trust. Note how those changes affect your relationship with your children.

→ **Remember . . .**

- When trust is the issue, sort out what is yours and own it.

- Projecting your issues onto your children invites retaliation.

- It takes a long time, much practice, and repetition to develop trust.

- Trust starts with your beliefs, not your children's behavior.

- When you do for your kids what they are able to do for themselves, you deprive them of a golden opportunity to develop self-trust.

- Your focal point in building trust is your children's potential and capability to learn step by step to take charge and to run their lives in a self-respecting and responsible manner. Your belief in them, even before they know the behaviors, brings out the best in them, cultivating trust.

- Understanding the value of being proactive with yourself first, and then your children, challenges you not to be shortsighted or omnipotent. Your children bloom better as you stand out of their light.

- Your peacefulness is your greatest asset, enhancing the development of trust.

**Chapter 4 Overview**

**Self-Esteem**

- What is Self-Esteem?
- The Degree to Which You Value Yourself is the Degree to Which You Value Your Children
- Why Self-Esteem is Important
- Self-Esteem is Learned, Not Inherited
- Self-Esteem is a Basic Psychological Need
- Your Self-Esteem Affects Everything You Do
- The Greatest Gift You Can Give to Your Children is Loving Yourself
- How Self-Esteem Develops
- You Change Your Self-Esteem by Changing Your Thinking
- For Your Journal
- Personal Empowerment is:
- Remember . . .

# 4

## Self-Esteem

### Self-Esteem:

- is based on your beliefs about yourself, not facts about you. The picture that you have of you may be quite different from the picture your child or others have of you.

- is the degree of love, acceptance, regard, respect, and valuing toward yourself in all areas of life.

- is synonymous with your very private and personal beliefs and attitudes about yourself. Some beliefs are conscious, some are subconscious, and all create feelings and behavior.

- is often confused with arrogance, vanity, smugness, audacity, haughtiness, conceit, insolence, and egotism which are cover-ups for a lack of, low, or negative self-esteem.

- is not static or fixed; it is in degrees. The degree to which you value and love yourself is the degree to which you love and value your children. You cannot give what you do not have, nor can you bypass yourself.

- is the greatest, not exclusive, characteristic that you and your children possess.

- is learned, not inherited, and at any point can be relearned or modified.

- is a basic psychological need. It is to your emotional well-being what food and water are to your physical well-being.

- needs that are not met are manifested in rude, disrespectful, controlling and disruptive behaviors. These behaviors invite from others the opposite of what is really needed. Rudeness invites rudeness, not love.

- that is high and positive, energizes; low self-esteem depletes physical and emotional energies.

- affords the opportunity for you to give your children the greatest gift of all—loving yourself.

- and self-respecting choices come from parents and kids who love and value themselves. Any errors that are made are seen as chances to learn and grow.

- gives you the right to say, "No one is as invested in me and my children as I am."

- is a process that begins to develop at birth and all through life. It affects every area of your human experience.

- develops in day-to-day ways of relating between you and your children. Reflections from you to your children say, "You are lovable and good" or "You are unlovable and bad."

- is changed by changing your thinking. Your thinking controls your beliefs; your beliefs control your feelings; and your feelings control your behavior.

- includes loving yourself as a choice in your thinking and knowing that you have all the resources you need within yourself. It is a choice to be your best friend or worst enemy.

- is enhanced as you accept behaviors that you do not like about yourself, then let go of them (change them). Denying behaviors that you do not like about yourself only intensifies those behaviors (makes change impossible).

- involves knowing that no one makes you feel inferior, worthless, or unloved unless you give another permission to do so.

## What is Self-Esteem?

Self-esteem asks one question: How much do I love, value, regard, accept, and respect myself? Self-esteem is the degree of loving, valuing, regarding, accepting, and loving that you have for yourself, all of which provide a base for your feelings and behaviors. What you believe about yourself is the same as the picture that you have of yourself; it is a picture that is based on belief, not fact. Your belief, how you feel about yourself, may have nothing to do with who you are or how others experience you.

Self-esteem is your private, personal beliefs and attitudes. Some of these beliefs and attitudes are conscious (known to you), others are subconscious (not known to you), all of these beliefs motivate your feelings and behaviors.

These beliefs were learned as a child when important adults, who from their own learned beliefs, spoke and related to you. In those interpersonal interactions you received messages that you interpreted as a statement about you. No one was there to teach you the third ground rule. **Each time I speak, I really am saying more about myself than I am saying about you, even though I attach your name to it.** Statements that you heard frequently became your beliefs about you. Now as a parent you relate to your children from your private belief system and the cycle continues.

Belief systems develop from what happens—life's experiences. For example, a mother, whose mother died when she was two-years-old, may feel frightened that her two-year-old will die and will be afraid to bond with and get emotionally close or will over-compensate by being over-protective. She might maintain distance by constantly criticizing or providing too strict or lenient limits, giving messages that can be interpreted by her daughter as, "I can't do it right," or "There is something wrong with me."

A father who was brutally beaten by his father may behave in ways to get his sons to like and validate him, thereby, providing no adult support and guidance for his sons. The message to his sons is "You have to be in charge and take responsibility for adults."

What happened to you as a child? Unless you have resolved the effects of the experiences, they continue to affect you first, and your children second. Your perception of your children is clearer than your view of yourself; the difference is the effect that your beliefs and feelings have on your perception—an effect which colors your view. In other words, you are more objective with how you see others than yourself.

The consequential question is how do you see yourself? What words do you use to describe you? Are they self-defeating or self-enhancing? You are always thinking; your on-going dialogue is with yourself. Many of your thoughts are never spoken out loud and include an evaluation about you, "How did I come across? Did I look stupid? Did what I said make sense? I wish I would have thought to say . . . . I felt so self-conscious and cannot remember what I did or said. I did that job well. I don't think I can handle this. I know I can . . . . I'll bet everyone thinks I am dumb."

This appraisal is more about you than your performance and achievement, even though a fine line separates who you are from your behaviors and accomplishments. In other words, you feel good or bad about what you do to the degree that you feel good or bad about who you are.

Defenses like arrogance, conceit, haughtiness, boasting, smugness, vanity, audacity, brazenness, pretense, and overconfidence invariably get confused with confidence and high self-esteem. The main purpose of the former is to mask a lack of and low self-esteem.

What is strong, high self-esteem, stands by itself. No pretense. Conversely, what is lacking or perceived as weakness requires a defense or cover-up.

Individuals in the privacy of the counseling relationship frequently reveal the incongruity between their feelings and their behaviors. For instance, clowning at a party covers the feeling of self-consciousness and invisibility. Being quiet and passive may appear to others to be insecurity or shyness when really a person is being peaceful and observant. Apparent calmness on the outside may cover a person's seething tensions inside.

Frequently, I hear parents say that they are providing certain things for their children to "give them self-esteem." Common offerings are dance, music, art, or martial arts classes, and membership in girl and boy scouts, 4-H groups, and summer camps. Skills gained from these experiences can enhance your child's feeling of mastery and competency to the degree that he/she already believes in him/herself. However, it is impossible to give self-esteem. It is yours. It belongs to you. Each individual, your children included, has his/her own. Self-esteem is individual, yet develops and is maintained interpersonally.

## The Degree to Which You Value Yourself is the Degree to Which You Value Your Children

The interrelatedness between trust and self-esteem was discussed in chapter three with emphasis on not bypassing yourself and knowing that you cannot give what you do not have. Your relationship with yourself affects your relationship with your children and others.

Parents are often puzzled by the fact that their relationships outside the family are different from relationships within the family; the contrast is the degree of importance of family versus others. In your secondary relationships with people outside the family, there is less at stake since they are not as important and invested in you. This in no way minimizes these connections; instead, it highlights the distinct dimension of the two relationships.

This implication increases the potential for acceptance and love, as well as rejection, and ridicule, leaving much at stake for self-esteem. What a paradox! The people who are closest to you can love or hurt you the most.

I hear parents say they cannot believe how their son acts when he is at other people's houses. "Well, you must be talking about another child; he doesn't act like that at home."

Contrasting the distinction between family and others is the existence of a different code of behavior and expectations for each. It is easier to be more consistently pleasant, patient, and kind with another's child. Your emotions and investment are so different with your own children. You can appreciate others' children for who they are, be more relaxed and objective, and see humor in their quirks and pet peeves. Is it possible to believe the old saying, "Treat company like family and family like company?" Is it just a myth? Can you imagine how our world would be different if one standard existed for all that underscored respect and peacefulness?

Understanding the relationship between you and your child's self-esteem is like putting on a pair of purple tinted glasses. All you see is purple. Change the color to orange; the world looks orange. Change to self-criticism; your tendency is to see others as critical. You and your choice of glasses determine what you see. It does not change what you are viewing. Pretending to see green through orange lenses is deceptive. You are the only one fooled. Your child can see the color of your glasses and loves you regardless of the color. The real question is: How much do you love and respect you? Are your glasses tinted with self-love or self-hate or something in-between?

Since self-esteem is yours and your child's greatest attribute, time given to learn and understand about it is of the essence. You cannot be too knowledgeable about the importance, development, and maintenance of this critical trait. It is one part of your life, totally in your control. You need to know the importance and effects of your beliefs.

## Why Self-Esteem is Important

### → Self-Esteem is Learned, Not Inherited

A common question I hear is "I want my child to have high self-esteem. I know I have very little. How can I give my child self-esteem?"

The following dialogue ensues in my office between the mother and father of Andrew, age seven, and me. I learn that Andrew's parents are delightful, intelligent, sensitive, and concerned individuals who need more coaching to learn to believe that each is a delightful, intelligent and concerned person.

Counselor: Many parents ask the same question. The answer is you cannot give self-esteem. That would be like giving your skin away. It belongs to you. Hence the word self. It all starts with you. Your level of respect and love for you determines the corresponding level of respect and love you have for your kids. You cannot water your garden with an empty watering can. That is simple and common sense. Yet at another level, it is not that simple. It takes slowing down the process and looking carefully at the interactions between you and your child; interactions that happen so quickly with seemingly little conscious thought.

First, what is going on inside you? Where is your level of self-love and respect at this moment? It can fluctuate momentarily; however, in general, you maintain a certain level.

Secondly, what are you saying with your words and behaviors? Thirdly, how do you think your child hears and receives what you say? Fourthly, how does your child respond?

Sounds tedious, I know. It is both complicated and simple. It is complicated if you do not see the individual steps. Can you afford not to pay meticulous attention to the most precious and consequential part of your parenting experience? Anything worthwhile takes much effort.

Back again to your question. What I hear by you asking the question is that you know self-esteem is important. If I understood you correctly, please give yourself credit. You deserve all the credit due you.

| | |
|---|---|
| Mother: | Well, never mind about me. I'm talking about Andrew, our seven-year-old son. I can tell he does not like himself. He even calls himself stupid and dumb. I don't know where he gets it. I never call him that. |
| Counselor: | Do you ever directly or indirectly call yourself stupid if you make a mistake or forget something? |
| Father: | I may think it or say it under my breath. Don't all parents do that? I am sure he doesn't hear me. Besides, we're talking about Andrew, not me. |
| Counselor: | At what times do you notice Andrew calling himself stupid? |
| Mother: | Well, he has high expectations for himself. If he doesn't do something perfect the first time, he says, "I'm stupid." I tell him he can't expect to get things perfect the first time he tries, and he won't listen. |

| | |
|---|---|
| **Counselor:** | Which one of you have high expectations for yourself and like to do things well, maybe the first time? |
| **Father:** | I guess we both do. We believe if you can't do it well, don't do it at all. That's what my dad told me all the time. |
| **Counselor:** | I am going to pretend I am Andrew for a minute. Please listen carefully. I know I am dumb and stupid. I see my mom and dad, the most important adults in my life, being able to do things so well and so fast. Every time I see something I want to do and I try it, if I don't get it perfect, I know again I am dumb and stupid. My mom tells me that I can't expect to get things perfect the first time. My dad keeps saying, "If you can't do it well, then don't do it at all." I've heard that a million times. I'll bet his dad said that to him too. My dad's words ring louder than my mom's. He is my male model. What a bind I am in. I have only lived for seven years and need practice to learn, so I can do things well. The only way to learn is to do and practice. Some of my little muscles are still developing and my eyes and hands are learning to work together. I sure work hard to get it right the first time. Honest, I do. I must really disappoint my dad, and I want to make him so proud of me. I am the first kid in our family. I am so dumb and stupid." |
| **Father:** | Do you think that is how Andrew feels? |
| **Counselor:** | Yes, I do. That is how I sense he is viewing your behavior and taking messages from you about him. He sees your behavior and hears your words clearly giving him instructions how to behave "If you can't do it well, then don't do it at all." There is no room for practice or mistakes. The message, "Do it as many times as you need to learn to do it well," would allow room for practice. When you give an opposite message, "You can't expect to be perfect the first time," after he |

feels he has failed, it is too contradictory and he cannot believe both. He hears the loudest and repetitive message. When he cannot do well on the first attempt, he feels like a failure; he diminishes himself, concluding that he is dumb and stupid. He will not doubt your word. You are his parent. Since he is young and depends on you, he believes that the inadequacy must be in him.

Father: So are you saying it (self-esteem) is picked up from me?

Counselor: Yes, you are absolutely right. Andrew's sense of himself, his self-worth, his self-respect, and self-responsibility are all learned, not inherited. Both your behavior and your words teach him. And, what is learned can be relearned and modified. No, it is not easy because it means that you need to change and relearn some behaviors; you are both VIP's (very important people) in Andrew's life. What you say and do impacts on him in a profound way.

Mother: That does make sense. I never thought about it in that way. Wow, I guess I need to listen to what I am saying to Andrew. That'll be tough.

Counselor: Yes, you are right. Before you can listen to Andrew, it might mean listening to what your parents said over and over to you that you are repeating to Andrew. You often speak without listening to yourselves, and your children hear every word you say and take them to heart, all affecting the development and maintenance of their self-esteem.

Father: That's scary.

Counselor: Yes, it is. It is also challenging. You pick the color of glasses you wear and the amount of water in your sprinkling can. Your child cannot do that. He is busy developing his own glasses or filling his own container. He is learning and forming his own beliefs and

attitudes that are his self-esteem. Self-esteem, in
addition to being learned, is also an emotional need.

### → Self-Esteem is a Basic Psychological Need

Self-esteem is to your emotional well-being what food and
water are to your physical well-being. It is the same as knowing the
difference in your child's behavior when he is hungry and tired as
opposed to when he is fed and rested.

The same is true with esteem-needs. Satisfy the needs and you
see visible results. Of course, as with food and sleep, meeting them
once is not enough. They need continual satisfaction until your
child is able to take over meeting her needs, a gradual process that
shifts from needing and wanting esteem and validation from others to esteeming and validating herself. It is also called being
grown-up, a journey she will be on 'til she dies.

If you observe and make comments about her behavior when
her need to be valued, or respected, or esteemed, or loved is
screaming to be gratified, what you see is just that. For example,
if you say, "Stacy sure is a brat today," what you are seeing is behavior that is saying, "Mommy, I am missing you and I need love
from you. So if I act up, you'll see I need some attention."

If you observe behavior when the need has been satisfied, the
behavior is the opposite of the unmet need. For example, after you
spend time with Stacy, her behavior changes, and she "becomes"
a delightful, good kid again. When esteem needs are not met to a
certain level of fulfillment, actions you label as rude, disrespectful,
controlling, manipulative, or disruptive become familiar and habitual.

Sadly and falsely, they become the child. Rude Kara. Controlling Greg. Bad Melissa. Obnoxious Zachary.

Unmet esteem-needs become behaviors that define and label,
are difficult to erase once ingrained, and are carried to adulthood.

Paradoxically, as a child or an adult, unmet needs invite from
others the opposite of what the person needs. The need gets lost
and camouflaged with defenses, hurt, compensatory behaviors,
and vindictiveness. Margie is an example of this.

## Margie

Margie was eleven months old when Elizabeth bumped her from the only-kid-position, one she coveted and wanted to occupy longer. Now that they are twelve and thirteen, Margie constantly feels intruded upon by her sister. Elizabeth borrows her clothes without asking and brings friends to the family room when Margie is reading.

Elizabeth has surpassed her in athletics. She runs faster on the tennis court, shoots more baskets, and makes more home runs.

How maddening! Doesn't Elizabeth know she was here first? Margie did not invite her.

Of course, Margie purposefully ignores the fact that she excels in music, drama, and creativity, thus compounding her feelings of being overwhelmed and crowded. Margie's constant focus on Elizabeth minimizes her strengths and accomplishments, serving to keep her rage and anger intact.

Every time Margie feels bumped or overpowered by her sister, she gets irate and verbally aggressive.

Her attacking, snappy, caustic, and critical replies do not invite what she is needing—which is positive recognition; ironically, the invitation is for the opposite. Criticism invites criticism. Anger invites anger. Verbal attacks invite verbal attacks.

It is difficult for Margie, her parents, and Elizabeth to see that Margie needs recognition that she is a wonderful person, even though her behavior is not so wonderful. Her parents can help her by defining and reinforcing rules about Elizabeth's borrowing from family members and using common living space. She also needs much assurance that there is enough room in her family for two intense, intelligent, high-achieving sisters who share similar developmental stages.

Her need for reassurance is greater when her behavior is rude and disruptive. Only seemingly contrary replies that humor or compliment her have the chance of meeting her unmet needs. Acceptance for criticism. Love for anger. Kindness for verbal attacks. What a challenge for her parents, for you as a parent!

Does that mean you need to be superhuman? Or are you saying you need to look at and change (as opposed to repeat) your behavior? Might this be a place to know peacefulness within yourself is your greatest asset?

As Margie's parents and other significant adults understand how she felt displaced by her sibling before Margie had reached her first birthday, they need to acknowledge what her behavior invites and respond with acceptance, understanding, respect, regard, patience, and love. They need to be persistent with their positive counter-replies; then old behaviors will be extinguished, and her self-esteem enhanced.

For her parents and you as a parent, this is a mammoth order and one that can be executed only by parents who have high levels of self-acceptance. Difficult, yes, and with practice, one's skill can be perfected. Remember, you control the color of your glasses. Margie's unmet needs affected her actions in every area of her life. Your unmet needs, as well as your child's, affect every area of your human experience.

## → Your Self-Esteem Affects Everything You Do

At first, this may sound like an outlandish, extreme statement. It is not! Your level of self-esteem is a powerful force filtering through every thought, feeling, and behavior.

Look closely at your motivation, your setting of realistic goals, your use of intelligence, and your choice of friends. Examine your level of self-responsibility, risk-taking, cooperation, initiative, self-monitoring, trust, creativity, openness, inquisitiveness, and spontaneity. All are directly and indirectly influenced by your attitudes about yourself.

As with other aspects of your life, it takes introspection and reflection to see the relationship. This connection is most perplexing when opposites exist between what you know to be your potential and what you see. Some typical examples are the following:

- The student with high intelligence and no learning disabilities who consistently gets failing grades.

- The teen with everything: good grades, many friends, success in sports, active in community projects, lifelong girl scout with every badge possible, attractive, and popular who attempts suicide.

- The father, supportive of his daughter's school, goes on field trips, volunteers in the classroom, is greatly appreciated by teachers, has the whole class to his house for her birthday, and helps his disabled neighbor with summer yard work who says he never does enough.

- The mother, always looking trim and neat, who says someone else looks better.

- The ten-year-old, frequently finding himself in the middle of a fight on the playground and never winning, who keeps going back for more fights.

For you as parents, when there appears to be no other explanations for comprehending these discrepancies, a look at self-esteem can provide a key for understanding behavior. Since you cannot look into your kid's head and heart, the alternative is to monitor your own inconsistencies. Only you know what goes on inside you. A trait, affecting all of your experiences, warrants much attention, affording you the golden opportunity of loving yourself; this is your greatest gift to your children.

## The Greatest Gift You Can Give to Your Children is Loving Yourself

There are no insurance companies that write policies to cover parenting. No agent says that if you pay this premium and if the unexpected happens, you will be reimbursed. No company tells you that you are not involved and what happens is out of your control.

The above is not surprising given the complexities of your on-the-job training and unknown outside influences. The closest you come to any guarantee is knowing that parents and kids who love and value themselves make self-respecting choices, and if they err, their mistakes are opportunities for learning and growth.

Since no one is as invested in you or your kids as you are, the greatest, longest-lasting gift you can give is for you to love yourself.

Loving yourself includes self-acceptance, self-respect, self-monitoring, and a willingness to forgive yourself when you make a mistake, even simple, obvious ones.

Many generations later will benefit even though you will never get the praise and thanks due you. This priceless gift costs no money, means your kids will not need to relearn who they are as adults, and can use the precious time for living a more fulfilled life. Yes, it involves you in a major way. The pay-off for you is greater peace and happiness. That is what you deserve.

## How Self-Esteem Develops

You as an infant are born with certain genetic endowments such as aptitude, height, eye and hair color, skin complexion, and personality predispositions. You have a birth rucksack with special pockets inside and outside. The largest item in the sack is a beautiful, clear slate. Quickly it starts to get filled in: who you are, how important you are, how competent you are, and how lovable, valuable, and worthwhile you are. Since you rely on significant people for care and protection, a mark is made on the slate from each interaction, in the previously stated areas, between you and the adult (parent).

I have a deep belief and prized assumption that all of us are born wonderful and lovely. An inside zippered pocket in our rucksack holds our own special birthright, entitling us to have all our needs fulfilled, become all we can, be protected from people who do not love themselves, be respected and loved even when we make mistakes, have our strengths emphasized, our weaknesses minimized, and be happy, joyful, and peaceful.

Since it takes some time for us to learn to reach into our rucksack pocket and read, adults in charge, usually parents, are counted on to assist. The first line of our birthright reads:

.noꙅɿɘd ɈnɒɈɿoqmi bnɒ ,ɘlidwdɈɿow ,ylɘvol ,luɟɿɘbnow ɒ ɘɿɒ uoY

Naturally, babies, cannot see themselves unless they are reflected in a mirror or someone serves as a mirror, leaving the only way the message can be read.

The other items in your birth rucksack are two separate zippered pockets. One says *For me*, the other *Against me*. For about five years, every first-hand interaction is analyzed to assess if it is a vote for or against you. Of course, you the infant and child do not know that your parent is echoing his/her beliefs and feelings at that moment; you think something is stated about you. This is your only option; you are dependent on your parents for your sense of yourself.

Somewhere around five-years-old, you become weary of examining each interaction. There are so many other things to do in the next thirteen to fifteen years. You need to master tasks of independence, vocation, relationships, and a life philosophy to serve as guidelines in all areas of your life. Looking into each pocket, you tally the number of votes. If the *For me* count is greater than the *Against me*, you conclude that I am lovable, wonderful, and valuable. If the votes in the *Against me* pouch are greater, the conclusion is I am unlovable, bad, and worthless.

These beliefs, which are different from facts, are the foundation for your self-esteem. These beliefs are stored in your subconscious (out-of-awareness). The main task of the beliefs is to control interactions by making sure there are no discrepancies. This means you can only pay attention to what others are saying about you if it fits what you already believe about yourself.

For example, you know people, who, when given a compliment, deflect or minimize it, by saying verbally or behaviorally, "You don't really mean that."

Unless you have reason to doubt the authenticity of the giver, you decide what happens to the commendation. Simply, will you believe it or not? If the compliment does not match your private belief system, it needs to be rejected. Congruence, not content, is focal. Two common examples illustrate this point.

Nate, who *is* and knows he is a wonderful cook, *believes* the rave reviews he gets from his dinner guests. Even if his guests do not like his cooking, he still believes he is a wonderful cook.

Cindy, who refinishes antiques with painstaking care and precision and does not believe she is skilled, refuses compliments, carefully pointing out flaws no one except she can see. No matter how many people are in awe of her work, she does not believe them. The picture she has of herself does not match the picture others have of her.

Other situations are less obvious, more complicated, and disguised like Carole's.

## Carole

The first time I met Carole, I was struck with both her inner and outer beauty. Her dark brown eyes glistened, accentuating her light brown complexion and dark curly hair that cascaded to her waist. I admired the gentleness and softness in her voice and manner as she detailed the last month, focusing on her five-year-old daughter Martha's night terrors. Both were exhausted and on edge. Neither had slept a full night in four weeks.

The pattern is predictable now. Mother gets apprehensive after dinner hoping in one breath that tonight will be different, yet assured in another breath that it will be the same. How long can she go with so little sleep? When will it end? What is going on for Martha? What is she doing wrong? How can she be such a horrible mother?

Martha and mother go through their established bedtime routine. Bath, brush teeth and hair, take stuffed animals from bed to cedar chest, tuck prized teddy bear in her bed, story, drink, toilet, and exchange, "I love you and good-night." Previously Martha fell asleep within ten minutes; now it takes thirty to forty-five minutes. Mother listens to the monitor in Martha's room and goes by her room every five minutes glancing in to see if she is asleep.

Once her daughter is asleep, mother collapses in sleep. At 12:30 a.m. Martha screams, interrupting both their sleep. As mother rushes to Martha's bedside, she is both scared and angry. Scared the pattern will continue forever and angry that her sleep is interrupted.

Martha is wide awake, sobbing, "I am so sorry."

Mother, not having pulled her defenses up since waking, sharply retorts, "Sorry for waking me?" Quickly her defenses mobilize, and she apologizes for snapping back.

Martha wants mother to sleep with her. Doing what it takes to get her back to sleep, mother lies down in Martha's bed, waits until Martha falls asleep, and then goes to her bed. At 4:00 a.m., as though an alarm were set, the pattern repeats.

Morning comes too quickly. Nothing is spoken about the night before. Both behave in apologetic ways by being overly polite. When the stress of the fatigue wears thin, irritability surfaces, followed by verbal promises to get along better. What is happening here?

Looking beyond the tiredness and frustration is the larger pattern of interruption, apology, interruption, apology. Why interrupt? Apologize for what? How is this related to self-esteem? What was Carole's relationship with her mother? Does she remember when she was five-years old?

Carole remembers when she was five and sadly enough has the same feelings about her mother as an adult that she had as a child. Carole's mother personalized (and still does) much of Carole's behavior. Whatever Carole does her mother interprets that as a statement about mother's behavior rather than realizing Carole has her own needs. Carole remembers wishing, as a child, that her mother would change. She now knows that as an adult she wanted her mother to love and respect herself more. She also knows now that wishing does not make changes in others.

Carole's mother felt most inadequate about herself. She never admitted it; unfortunately, how she acted was the proof. Her mother's belief toward herself is I am inadequate. The fact is that she is very adequate and has many abilities and skills. Her belief is the opposite.

Mother's best defense and form of compensation is to interfere and apologize. "Let me do it for you. You can't do that like that. What did you do that for? You don't know how to do this? That will never work. Where did you get your crazy idea? You never do anything right. I know you'll goof this one."

Carole's response, from her own need to learn and gain independence, was typical of any kid. "I can do this. Yes, I can. I want to do this all by myself. I don't need any help. Let me alone!"

The bottom line for Carole: Stop interfering, or I will find a way to get you back. I know what I need.

Mother's personalization (saying Carole was talking about her rather than Carole's developmental needs) was support for her belief. "See, she won't let me help her or do it for her. I am inadequate."

Parents personalize their children's behavior to the degree that they do not have a positive, accepting sense of themselves. They lack clear, respectful, personal boundaries defining what is and is not theirs. Their child is to complete the lack of wholeness they feel. A sure way children can protect or maintain what is theirs is to cave in, fight back, or get back.

Mother, feeling threatened by her young daughter's emerging independence, would retort with, "Well, I can't do anything right," (I am inadequate). She was totally personalizing what was said and rejecting her daughter. Then mother would top it off with a hostile and terse, "I am sorry," as in sorry for the inconvenience of being alive, as if Carole had anything to do with that.

Carole, scared about losing emotional ties with mother, apologized for being a bad girl even though she was simply being a kid and put another vote in her *Against me* pouch, reinforcing the emerging belief that she was inadequate and bad. After all, she could not do it right and please mother the adult; she was the kid; it must be something about her. Then mother would apologize after seeing how dejected Carole felt perpetuating the interference and apologies pattern.

Interference was her mother's preferred way of proving her private belief of inadequacy. The behavior Mother chose was less important than the meaning it had for Mother; to her it proved she was inadequate. Part of the meaning came from how mother viewed (personalized) Carole's response to Mother's interfering.

Carole had the option of selecting her best way of getting back. It is not surprising that she chose what was modeled for her, interference followed by apologies. For example, the pattern went like this: Carole would not listen to her mother the first time. She waited until mother was involved in a task to say that she needed her mother's time. Mother would get furious, and this was followed by Carole's apology.

Also, Carole refused to have eye contact with mother when she was talking, creating an interference in their communication. Carole waited until the last minute to let Mother know when she needed something for school or Girl Scouts. When she was older, Carole withheld information and interrupted mother's plan of being in charge. This was followed by apologies of "I forgot."

Neither mother nor daughter understood the power, impact and challenge of parental modeling.

Carole's wholesome young child assertiveness threatened her mother's chosen defense of overpowering and interfering, covering up her "I am inadequate" belief.

Long ago Carole had convinced herself that she was in no way like her mother; however as she shared her story, she began to waiver on her conviction.

Recognizing, revering, and, in the true sense honoring the power and impact and challenge of parental modeling, Carole realized that she was doing the same interfering with Martha. Carole was overprotecting, overmonitoring, overstructuring Martha.

Martha's chosen form of retaliation was the same as her mother and grandmother's. Martha interrupted her mother's sleep. Martha's choice, not conscious, emerged from her need to protect herself and in another way at another level, not to be too different than her mother and grandmother.

*The apples do not fall very far from the tree.*

As Carole recognized the pattern and the connection to her private beliefs about herself, she could change. She chose to monitor her interfering behaviors, catching herself each time. When she found herself in the middle of interrupting, she said to Martha, "I don't want to do that. That is my old way. I do not want to interfere with what you are capable of doing."

Carole would start over. Consequently, Martha knew that her mother was in control of herself and not controlling the situation, a distinct difference.

Carole needed to clarify what was legitimate parental guidance and what was interfering. Her determining probe was the answer to the question, "Is this a task or responsibility Martha can do herself, or is it my old defense to prove my old inadequacy belief?" If she could answer with an honest *Yes*, she let go. If *No*, she provided the limits, structure, support, training, and cuing that Martha needed.

Learning this critical difference allowed Carole to reclaim a belief in herself that was sidetracked when she was a child. The difference also afforded her the responsibility of changing her belief and deepening her own self-respect, regard, and esteem.

Additionally, Carole worked from the inside out by saying over and over, "I am a wonderful, lovely and adequate person." Even though it sounded and felt phony, initially, the repetition convinced and retrained her. Needless to say, Martha and her children-to-come are beneficiaries.

Given the complexity of being a parent, the training on-the-job that never ends, and the external influences that are out of your control, you as parents need to find something constant and consistent to serve as an anchor, which is your thinking and your beliefs.

Why are the most simple, obvious facets in your control overlooked? It is similar to appreciating the electricity when it is on rather than when it is off, or listening to what you know is best rather than giving in when you are questioned by your child, or remembering that you are the least aware of how you are feeling when you are the most irritable.

Why do you tend to give your power to people and events outside yourself? For instance, you assume that someone in an authority role (doctor, supervisor, principal, teacher) knows more right answers about you and your child than you know. When you give power to the outside, your thinking and the control you have over your thinking get nullified. This becomes another learned way of working against yourself.

## You Change Your Self-Esteem
## By Changing Your Thinking

When you become an adult, you are in charge of your self-esteem. Taking charge is a gradual process from your birth to now. It is your birthright. To change your self-esteem, you need to change your thinking. Your thinking controls your beliefs (I am inadequate); your beliefs control your feelings (I feel inadequate); your feelings control your behavior; (I behave in ways that show my inadequacy: I am always goofing up, I never do anything right because I rush too much and am not careful, I sabotage myself by not being on time for important events). You are like an iceberg with your behavior seen by others, and your beliefs and feelings hidden under the surface, known only to you.

Since self-esteem is learned, both yours and your child's, it can be relearned and modified. As opposite as it appears, accepting what you do not like, allows you to let go. Rejecting what you do not like, intensifies it. In other words, when you accept your perceived faults and weaknesses, the act of acceptance helps you to change. "I accept that I am critical much of the time. I know I am. It is a behavior I can change." When you reject a fault you have, the act of rejecting makes you deny that behavior. You spend energy covering up and defending. "I am never critical. I am not! Not me." Your focus is on ways to protect yourself from how other see you behave.

The following technique can help you to break self-defeating patterns.

### → For Your Journal (A Simple Self-Enhancing Exercise)

It takes monitoring just like you watch your fuel tank gauge for you to be in charge of and enhance first, your self-esteem, and second your child's self-esteem. Remember, that is the only order. In your journal, create a new section. Select a title such as:

> *What I Do For Myself*
> *For Me*
> *My Self-Esteem Gauge*
> *My Strengths And Weaknesses*
> *Wonderful Me*
> *I Am Important*
> *Loving Me More*
> *VIP*
> *I'm Responsible For Me*

The title you select may feel awkward, yet your feelings of awkwardness will change with time.

On the first page of this section, write the heading, "Strengths and Pluses." Then write a list of your strengths, quickly putting down what comes to mind, such as flexible, hard-working, sensitive, creative, high-energy, candid, kind, intuitive, honest, and dependable. Record what you believe your strengths are, not what others say.

Refrain from scrutinizing or picking apart what comes to mind such as, "Well, sometimes, I mess up and am not candid." You can easily find exceptions, no doubt, without looking far. The idea is to give yourself the benefit of the doubt. If you are candid much of the time, write that down. See this as an on-going log about your relationship with you. You live closer to yourself than anyone else. Write what comes readily to you. Let your thinking be candid.

Since this might be a foreign way of your thinking about yourself, be patient and gentle. If you have a hard time thinking about your strengths, list things you do well.

If you are good at calligraphy, identify the traits and characteristics you have that make you proficient. Are they a steady hand, excellent spatial relationships and fine motor coordination, appreciation for fineness, meticulousness, patience, and perseverance? Write them down.

If you are a good host or hostess, you no doubt are outgoing, pleasant, sensitive, able to carry on an interesting conversation, good at organizing, and flexible. Add these to your list.

Do not be concerned about your selection of what you do well and what the connection is to parenting. The traits and characteristics you possess relate to all areas of life.

After you list your strengths, skip some pages in your journal for future entries and begin a section entitled, "Weaknesses or Liabilities." Again, list what comes to mind that you believe are your minuses. Be specific, entering stubborn, lazy, insensitive, and rigid. It is possible to have the same trait in each section. Sometimes your stubbornness is an asset, other times a liability. It is a plus when you stubbornly stick to your word that you know is best for your child and not be swayed by his testing. It becomes a minus when you stubbornly refuse to listen when you have erred, need to back off, and apologize.

Daily, weekly or monthly, or sometime in between, continue making entries in each section. Date each time you write. Think about who you are. You, and only you are in charge of your self-esteem.

Be flexible with your entries. Know that you can change, learn to respect and value yourself more, and from time to time delete what does not fit. Change what is fitting to be changed in your plus and minus sections. Only you can change your weaknesses into strengths.

Write daily and/or weekly observations about what you have been thinking in terms of your strengths and weaknesses, how much you love or hate yourself, what you say to yourself in the privacy of your thinking, and what you are learning about yourself. Read and re-read your entries. Challenge yourself to focus more on your strengths. This is a simple way for you to take control of your self-esteem. As you change your thinking, your beliefs, your feelings, and eventually your behavior toward yourself and your child, then your child will follow suit. The benefit of increased self-esteem is yours and your child's.

→ **Personal Empowerment is:**
- believing you can and do make a difference; bringing out the best in yourself and your children;

- believing you can change your history rather than repeat it;

- knowing your Achilles heel and not personalizing what others are saying;

- believing there is a direct relationship between the degree of regard for yourself and your children;

- excluding judgments and criticism (self and others), anger, fear and guilt;

- knowing that you control your thinking;

- sharing peace, serenity, and love from one lovely human being to another;

- creating and maintaining a process within yourself;

- accepting what you have and do not have control over;

- doing small things in a big way until you are able to do big things in a wonderful way;

- accepting the only two choices you have—love or fear;

- being peaceful at all times;
     *being peaceful . . .*
          *being peaceful . . .*
               *being peaceful . . . .*

→ **Remember . . .**

- The difference between fact and belief cannot be emphasized too much.

- Who you are as a wonderful, valuable, worthy, and capable person is in contrast to what you believe.

- Since your beliefs are so strong, they feel like facts to you. You are functioning as though it were fact.

- It is amazing how individuals tenaciously hang on to their beliefs even in light of stellar accomplishments.

- Truly, belief is the meaning you give to you and what you do.

- Claim the personal power that was rightfully given to you at your birth. That is what you deserve, as do your children.

**Chapter 5 Overview**

**Respectful Communication in the Parent-Child Relationship**

- **What is Respectful Communication?**
- **Respect Does Not Necessarily Mean Agreement**
- **What You Say Might be Different from What Your Child Hears**
- **Is it a Question or a Statement?**
- **Respectful Communication is Intrapersonal and Interpersonal: Words, Behaviors, Gestures, and silences Say What is Happening Inside You and Between You and Your Child**
- **The Two Roles: Presenter and Receiver**
- **Respectful Communication: Potential for Emotional Closeness**
- **Process is Primary to Content**
- **Words Once Said Have Impact**
- **Paraphrasing: A Powerful Communication Tool**
- **For Your Journal**
- **Remember . . .**

# 5

# Respectful Communication in the Parent-Child Relationship

## Respectful Communication:

- is a form of dialogue with your children where both of you share your needs, wishes, and feelings in a way that enhances trust, integrity, and emotional intimacy.

- is a learned skill that takes much practice to perfect.

- involves the processes of appreciation, honesty and consistency.

- does not necessarily mean agreement; it means understanding what the other person said.

- is a goal in your relationship with your children; reaching this goal means knowing that what you say might be different from what your children hear.

- involves knowing the difference between asking a question and making a statement. Your children hear the difference and respond accordingly.

- is intrapersonal and interpersonal. You are always communicating with yourself (internal dialogue) or with your children (external dialogue). Words, behaviors, and silences say what is happening inside you and between you and your child.

- includes two roles: the presenter and the receiver. You can only be in one role at a time. Confusion results if you attempt to be in both roles at the same time.

- provides the potential for emotional intimacy, feeling close and connected when physically apart.

- includes the process of openness, cooperation, and love which is primary to the content (what the topic is). Defensiveness, discord, and anger are absent.

- involves knowing that words once spoken have impact. It takes longer to retract a word's impact than not to say it in the first place.

- includes using *can't, but,* and *why* with caution. *Can't* denotes helplessness, *but* cancels or minimizes what was said before the *but,* and *why* poses impossible questions for children to answer. In place of *can't* use *will not, choose not to,* or *do not want to.* In place of *but* use *and* or make two simple sentences. In place of *why,* use *what, where, when, who* or *how.*

- includes the use of paraphrasing to foster understanding. Paraphrasing is a powerful communication skill as outlined in the following steps.

→ **Guidelines For Paraphrasing: Seven Steps**

(1)

Q. How are you feeling?

A. Loving, scared, tense, peaceful, impatient, or patient?

(2)

Q. How do you think your child is feeling?

A. The importance is your timing in talking to your child.

(3)

Q. What is the issue or topic?

A. Be specific. An example is doing homework, taking care of personal items, use of the telephone, and fighting with her brother.

(4)

Q. What message do you want your child to receive?

A. Usually it is a message that your child needs to hear in order to develop more self-responsibility.

(5)

Q. What is the clearest way that you can state your message?

A. You cannot be too specific in your own mind. Do not focus on agreement, or you will become defensive. Your message will sound controlling and will invite defensiveness. Be very specific and state your message.

(6)

Q. Ask your child, "What did you hear me say?"

A. Listen carefully to what your child heard you say. If what you said was heard by your child, acknowledge the message. Say, "Yes, that is exactly what I said." If part of your message was received exactly, acknowledge that part. Say, "You heard what I said about . . .; I also said . . ." If part of your message was distorted, say, "No, I did not say . . .; What I said was . . . ." Do this as often as is needed until your message is received by your child in the way that you said it. Stay patient as you restate your message and wait for your child to hear (not agree with) what you said.

(7)

Work out a plan and any necessary details. Reflect on the process and what was accomplished.

### → A Respectful Communication Oath

*When my communication is respectful, that is, clear, with careful timing and paraphrasing, I spend more time in the short run, and less time in the long run conveying my message. My words and behavior have impact and influence that cannot be retracted.*

## What is Respectful Communication?

Respectful communication is a form of dialogue, listening and responding, with your children where both of you share requests, needs, wishes, wants, ideas, and feelings in a way that enhances trust, esteem, integrity, and emotional intimacy. It is a learned skill that takes much time to perfect. It does not mean agreement; the emphasis is on understanding what the other person is saying and means. Like trust and esteem-building, respectful communication is another way that you can foster respect and peacefulness.

Respect is the process of regarding, valuing, considering, recognizing, and appreciating. It is being genuine, kind, courteous, open, honest, fair, equitable, tolerant, and consistent.

Respect is a psychological need. All of you, no matter what your age, want to be recognized, esteemed, appreciated, valued, listened to, and heard. You want to be given consideration for your thoughts and point of view, especially by the people who care about you.

What is communicated in an atmosphere of respect provides safety, trust, and freedom to be yourself; respect is fostered. Respect, like trust and love, grows slowly. Respect, like trust and love, teaches and invites the same.

When respect is difficult to cultivate, there is often confusion about the difference between respect and agreement.

## Respect Does Not Necessarily Mean Agreement

There can be respect without agreement; respect and agreement are not always the same. You know adults whom you highly respect, yet you do not always agree with them.

Respectful communication is understanding what was said even when you have a different opinion or perspective. I hear parents confusing the two concepts and saying to their children, "You are not respecting me," with a hidden and unspoken message, "You are not agreeing with me." If agreement is what you want, say, "You are not agreeing with me."

On the other hand, I have heard parents, who know the difference say, "I don't agree with your choice, yet I respect the decision you made." At least, your acknowledgement is honest and open—a condition that fosters respect. Respect is too important to be confused with agreement.

Your children have so much going on with their own development that the message they receive from your communication may be very different from what you said. Your message is received through the filter of your children's thoughts and feelings.

## What You Say Might Be Different From What Your Child Hears

How often do you say something to your child that he hears very differently from what you said? For instance, your eight-year-old son is responsible for feeding his dog. You notice that his dog's water bowl is empty. You remind your son about the bowl. He responds with, "You don't think that I can do anything right." He heard and interpreted your reminder knowing that he was remiss in taking care of his dog.

As you think about the original question, you can feel the frustration that accompanies this communication break-down. Then there are those times when your child hears and receives your message the way you mean it. What makes the difference? Is it you? Is it your child? Is it both of you? How often do you stop to figure out what is happening? Do you reflect on this question when you are feeling frustrated or peaceful? Are your answers the same or different at these times? Do you think more about what is happening in you or what you see your child doing?

What conclusions have you drawn about you and your child's communication styles and patterns? Are the conclusions observations or beliefs?

Your observation is an awareness and recognition of the interpersonal dynamics in a situation that includes room for flexibility and change. This is what I see happening. Your beliefs imply acceptance about the interpersonal dynamics in a situation, acceptance that continues to create the same behaviors unless your views are changed. This is how it is.

The following are some observations that parents share with me:

- When I talk with my son when he is overly-tired or involved in an activity, he seems to ignore me and what I say.

- When my daughter is rested and not preoccupied, she is more attentive to what I say.

- When I am stressed and rushed, my message I want to share comes out differently from when I am rested and relaxed.

- Sometimes I am unsure about what I want to say, so how could my children get my message.

- When I take time to think first and my thoughts are clear, my daughter listens.

- Some common beliefs parents share are:

- I am never listened to; I might as well talk to a wall.

- I wasn't listened to as a child and nothing is different now.

- My children never hear a word I say; I have to yell before I am heard, and then I feel like I am out-of-control.

- What I have to say doesn't matter.

- Communication with my kids (and others) is hard work.

Sometimes, both observation and belief are present in an interaction. In the following example, Michael's mother first reacted from belief: (I know that I told him to buy a small bag of pretzels; he never listens to me) then switched to an observation: (He listened to me; my communication excluded what he was thinking).

Michael's mother sent him to the store to buy milk and bread. To show her thanks for the favor, she told him that he could buy a bag of pretzels. She allotted money for a small bag and told him that she was expecting back a certain amount of change. When Michael returned home eating and enjoying a big bag of pretzels, his mother was furious and accused him of not listening and not obeying. As Michael pulled the correct change from his pocket that mother anticipated, she asked him where he got the extra money for the more expensive treat. Michael clearly stated that he spent the exact amount of money allotted him and used his own money. He said, "You did not say that I could not use my money." As his mother thought back about what she actually said, she realized that Michael heard and did exactly what she said.

What you are thinking and want to say or have said is coming from your thoughts and experiences. How your children hear you is filtered through their thoughts and experiences. Is it any wonder that respectful communication exists in any relationships? And yes, like anything else that is valuable and worthwhile, it is hard work. Part of that hard work involves listening to yourself and knowing when you want to ask a question or make a statement.

## Is It a Question or a Statement?

Young children (early elementary grades) are in a concrete stage of development and hear and interpret what you say in a literal way. If you ask a question, that is what they hear. If you make a statement, that is what they hear. Asking your four-year-old, when it is time to sleep, "Do you want to go to bed?" will surely bring an answer of "No." Your son heard a question and answered it. Saying, "It is bedtime, and I want you to go to bed" might bring a "no" response (his assertiveness and independence), yet it eliminates the confusion between a question and a statement.

Use a question when your child truly has an option to make the decision and when you are open to listen to and to accept her response without reservation. Make sure your child has the maturity to make the choice that you are asking. This is a common oversight for first-time parents. From your lack of experience, you offer too many choices to your first-born too early. Too many choices overload your child before he/she is capable of undertaking that level of responsibility.

Use a statement when you know what is best for your child and when there is no choice. When I point out this difference, parents tell me that they assume by asking a question, rather than stating what needs to happen, they are being nice. When parents are nice by asking questions, children often see this as parents manipulating them. My response is, "Know that you already are nice. Manners are a separate topic."

Understanding what is reasonable for different developmental stages assists you in discerning when to ask questions or make statements. What is reasonable for a two-year-old may be unreasonable for an eight-year-old. If you do not already have one, purchase a book on developmental stages and tasks of children so you can become acquainted with what is reasonable for the stage that your child is in right now.

Sometimes parents and other adults mix statements and questions. The most common is making a statement then adding the question OK. For example, "I want you to stop teasing your sister. OK? I will come and help you in a minute. OK?" Do you think that your daughter is going to answer, "Of course, Dad, I agree. I do want to stop teasing my little sister." Or will your son say, "For sure, Mother, it is fine with me if you help me whenever you can. Take as many minutes as you need. I am a very patient child." You can see that these are most unlikely responses.

The question after the statement says that your child has a choice. Is there really a choice? Again, the OK should not be a way of sounding polite to cover a direct statement or a request that you assume your child might not like to hear.

Older children also hear and know the difference between a question and a statement. They hear your literal message and also hear what you are not saying, that is, what you are implying. Your statement, that you think is clear (and is to you), can be heard by your child in another way, as was true for Michael and his pretzels. Keep in mind that respectful communication is both intrapersonal (within you) and interpersonal (between you and your children).

## Respectful Communication is Intrapersonal and Interpersonal: Words, Behaviors, Gestures, and Silences Say What is Happening Inside You and Between You and Your Child

You are always communicating with yourself and your children. Words, behaviors, gestures, and silences say what is happening within and between you. You have an on-going internal dialogue that affects your communication with your children. As your internal communication is respectful, so is your external communication. As your internal communication is disrespectful and critical, so is your external communication. Respectful communication begins with you.

Communication is not limited to speaking words. Silence can say: I want to be alone, I need time to think, I need time to cool down and get control, I need privacy, I do not want to talk now, I am hurt, I am angry, I want to punish you, I'm thinking of a way to get you back, I want to punish myself, I am thinking, or I am enjoying this peaceful moment. Silence can punish, destroy, support, heal, or comfort.

However you choose to feel or behave at a given moment, you are telling the other person what is happening inside you. Words may disguise your experience by projecting blame on the other person when you say, "You made me mad" rather than "I am very angry and upset now." Projection is a way of blaming the other person for what is going on inside you; then you do not have to take responsibility for what is happening within you. Nonetheless, you are talking about you. When you choose to be honest with yourself and not project blame, you model for your children the importance of taking responsibility for what is going on inside them.

Your facial expressions, gestures, and behavior also communicate. You have seen looks that kill and have felt a hug that melted your heart. The messages vary from: come close to me or stay away, I love you or I hate you, you are my friend or you are my enemy, I want to talk or I want to be quiet, I want help or I do not want help, or I want to help you or I do not want to help you.

Whatever the mode of expression you use to communicate, you function sometimes as the presenter and sometimes as the receiver.

## The Two Roles:
## Presenter and Receiver

There are always two roles in the communication process; a presenter and a receiver. Both roles employ decoding—understanding what the message is and what the message means. This is a challenge for all ages and developmental stages.

Messages are transmitted so quickly that the line between presenter and receiver gets blurred. You switch back and forth from receiving what your child is saying to presenting your response. Respect is present when the topic stays the same throughout the conversation, each listens until the other is finished talking with no interrupting, and both are honest within themselves.

Sometimes one person will stay in both roles switching back and forth. This is most obvious when the question asked is answered by the same person in the same breath as in the following examples.

- "Do you want to go to the park? No you cannot go; you have homework to do."

- "Do you understand me? I can tell you don't."

- "You don't care, do you? That is obvious."

- "Do you want to go to your room? I can see you do."

- "Do you want everyone to make fun of you? You sure must if you wear that outfit."

It is similar to playing a game of tennis all by yourself, hitting the ball in one court and running frantically to the other side to hit it back. When you think about how funny this looks, hogging the court is also disrespectful and exhausting. This applies to both primary (family) and secondary (outside the family) relationships.

Have you ever started a sentence and someone finished it for you without your permission? Or you were adamantly told what you were thinking without a chance to speak? Both are common, enraging, and disrespectful.

Obviously, children who have acquired language can verbalize their needs and wants more readily than children without language. By crying and fussing, infants present their needs, and you receive their messages even though you are unclear about what is happening inside them. Using trial and error, you present back to them what you think you heard them convey to you. I will change your diaper. Does that make you comfortable? I will burp you and hope that releases the gas bubble in your stomach causing distress. I will hold you and provide warmth and closeness. I will feed you. Is that satisfying? Your young child's sense of satisfaction as seen in his calmness and serenity says, "I received your message through your action, you are correct, and I am feeling listened to and comforted. Thank you."

You employ the same decoding when your six- or sixteen-year-old son says, "When is dinner?" He is not casually asking when dinner will be ready so he can plan the next two hours of his day. His message, "I am starved," is hidden. "Mom, what do you have planned for this afternoon?" might mean, "I want a ride to my friend's house, or Can I have a friend come to my house?"

Behavior communicates a message as the mother of thirteen-year-old Cara discovered when she read the open note her daughter left on the kitchen counter. It was from Cara's girlfriend stating details about crawling out of her bedroom window that night after the family was asleep. Her friend was asking Cara to do the same. The message Cara received from her friend was so scary that she needed help from her parent, yet she was afraid that if she was direct that her friend would get in trouble. Giving the message indirectly, by leaving the note open and in an obvious place where her parent could see it, was her way of asking for help.

When you are in a conversation with your children, sometimes that means waiting for them to hit the ball back. Your patience and silence communicates respect for the time they need to think and reply—respect that enhances emotional closeness between you and your children.

## Respectful Communication: Potential For Emotional Closeness

The parent-child relationship, like primary adult relationships, has the potential for emotional closeness. Feelings of closeness provide connectedness when you are physically near or apart. The closeness comes from the images you carry in your head and the feelings that follow when you think about your child. The same goes for your child. The degree of respect in your communication exchanges and patterns affect the level of closeness.

Emotional closeness is feeling safe, wanted, protected, connected with, comfortable, trusted, and valued. As with trust and self-esteem, this closeness takes place in interpersonal exchanges between you and your child.

Exchanges from day one even before language develops to adult conversations communicate needs, feelings, and wants. Some are obvious and clear; others are subconscious and disguised. Whatever the form, a need is presented and requires a response, an answer of some kind.

Emotional closeness is present in your dialogues when either or both you and your child are respectful of yourself and each other. What you are discussing is less important than your respectful attitude. In other words, you need to know and understand the difference between process and content.

## Process is Primary to Content

Process is stepping back and looking at the whole forest while content is bumping your nose against a single pine tree.

Content is the topic being talked about. Process is what is happening between two people; one or both are being hostile, cooperative, defensive, loving, or disrespectful. Process is the big picture (forest) while content is part of the picture (tree).

The process is always primary to the content. Process is the atmosphere determining how the topic will be shared, compromised, or resolved. Process is experienced in your feelings; content is experienced in your thinking.

As crucial as any topic might be, if it is discussed in an adversarial atmosphere, the topic will be affected. If discussed in an atmosphere of openness, love, and cooperation, respect will grow even if you have dissimilar views. Even though the process (the larger picture) is more primary than the content (the words spoken), words do have their own effect.

## Words Once Said Have Impact

The moment a word or words leave your mouth there is influence and impact that cannot be retracted. Your child heard what you said and is affected by your words. It takes less time to stop and think before speaking than it takes to deal with the impact of words you said that you wish you would not have said.

Individual words can change the entire message your child hears in addition to enhancing or destroying respect. Three such words are: *can't, but,* and *why.* There appears to be a double standard with their usage in that it is more permissible for parents to use them than children. For example, I have heard parents say; "I *can't* do that now. *Can't* you see I am busy?"

Where is the double standard? You can see it by asking yourself if you have ever said this to your child? Was this a way that your parents related to you? And what would you do if your child said this to you? Doing away with double standards creates understanding and respect.

The more honest and respectful words are:

"*I will not* do that now. I know you can see that I am busy." You can talk in this way to young children, even though it appears that they do not understand the words. They do understand your tone of voice and feel your respect.

*Can't* denotes inability, helplessness, and victimization. For instance, if you say to your child,

"I can't come out and see the frog you caught now. I am getting dinner." Your child's response is, "Yes, you can. You can (are capable) come out." A self-respecting response is, "I am preparing dinner now. I can do one important thing at a time. Ask me another time." In place of *can't,* substitute *will not, choose not, do not want to, or am not free or available at this time.*

*But* is a mighty word hooking two sentences together. Invariably, both sentences are significant and true. The way your child receives each message when you use *but* is important. Your message preceding the *but* is negated or minimized by what follows. In other words, what comes after the *but* is heard by your child as more important than what is said before the *but.* It is most confusing when responses are mixed with love or trust. For example, "I trust you, *but* I do not want you to go downtown alone." Do you trust her? If yes, reword your statement and say, "I trust you. I do not want you to go downtown alone." If trust is not an issue, simply say, "I do not want you to go downtown alone."

If love is connected with your message, say so clearly so each has the chance of being heard. If you say, "I love you, *but* I wish you would be more careful," your statement of love might be overshadowed by the "be more careful" message. Instead say, "I love you and I wish you would be more careful." The message here is since you love her you want her to be more careful. Hearing your love might help her to be more careful.

When you have a tendency to use *but,* you can listen more carefully to what you say by asking yourself if both messages are important. If they are, make two simple sentences or use *and* in place of *but.* Both have the chance of being heard equally, and you invite less defensiveness.

*Why* is another word that needs to be used with caution. Most *why* questions that adults ask children are impossible to answer. Children feel inadequate when they are not able to answer adults' questions. Most *why* questions are asked when parents are feeling angry or frustrated about their child's behavior. *Why* is more appropriately used when probing topics other than behavior. The following are common *why* questions.

"*Why* did you get your shoes wet?" Do you think your three-year-old is going to say, "I just thought it would be fun, I wanted to make more work for you, or I wanted to see how it felt."

"*Why* did you forget your homework?" Unlikely answers are "If you are taking responsibility for it, there's no reason for both of us to remember, I want to give you something to be upset about, I only remember what is important to me, and You keep telling me that I have a terrible memory."

"*Why* did you spill your milk?" Doubtful responses are "You say I am a klutz, I was goofing around and did not watch what I was doing, or I was being careless."

"*Why* did you lie to me?" Do you think any child would say, "I am learning to fool myself and you, I am a liar, I want to be deceptive, I painted myself into a corner and it was the only way out." Your child's most probable answer is "I dunno" and a feeling of stupidity not to be able to answer your question.

Substitute *who, what, where, when* and *how* for *why.* These questions can be answered, giving the responsibility for actions back to the child where it belongs. For example say,

"Where did you get your shoes wet? When did you get your shoes wet? How did you get your shoes wet? What were you doing when your shoes got wet?

"What were you thinking about when your teacher gave the homework assignment? Where were you when your teacher gave the homework assignment? When did your teacher give the homework assignment? How much time does your teacher spend giving the homework assignment? What do you do when your teacher gives the homework assignment?

"What were you doing when your milk spilled? How did your milk spill? Where do you need to keep your hands and feet so your milk doesn't spill again? Who spilled your milk? What do you want to use to clean up your spilled milk? What needs to happen now that your milk is spilled?

"What were you thinking about when you lied to me? Whom were you with? What did you think I would say if you told me the truth? How did you think I would not find out the truth? Where were you when it happened? How scared were you? What did you want to happen? What kind of a bind were you in? How much time did you spend thinking about what would happen?"

All of these questions have a chance of being answered, even by young children. When children can answer your questions because there is a response that makes sense to them, they feel more competent and more in charge of their behavior. Your communication messages can never be too clear or too simple. To help you to become more sensitized to these three words, write them in bold black letters and put a red X through them. Put them on your refrigerator. Also list the following steps of paraphrasing to help your communication be more respectful.

## Paraphrasing:
## A Powerful Communication Tool

Communications can be enhanced by using a common sense technique called paraphrasing, a way of communicating that safeguards against misunderstandings and enhances respect. Breakdowns occur as conclusions get drawn about what "I thought I heard you say . . .," or "It sounded like that to me." Remember, each person has his/her own individual meaning about what is said and heard. Because it is so clear to you, does not mean it is clear to your child.

Paraphrasing is a simple communication tool that includes stating a message clearly, listening for understanding, and responding to what is stated to be sure the message is heard in the way the presenter intended. Listening for what was said, to the presenter's satisfaction, and not looking for agreement sets the stage for understanding as opposed to defensiveness, rebuttal, and argument.

Paraphrasing is especially useful for topic areas where there is a difference of opinion. It helps in those areas where you feel out-of-charge, or where there is continual conflict. To illustrate paraphrasing, you will be taken through the seven steps using the common situation of kids not picking up after themselves. In order for you to be effective at paraphrasing, the following ideas are preparation for the seven steps.

Respectful communication takes more time in the short run and less time in the long run. It is critical to pick a time when you are not rushed. Rehearse the seven steps so they are clear in your mind. Remember, you cannot be too clear, specific, and focused. Start out by saying, "I have something very important to talk about."

Then follow the seven steps of the paraphrasing process.

### → Ask Yourself

1. *"How am I feeling?"* Is it loving, relaxed, scared, tense, open, defensive, angry, or sad? How you are feeling colors what you say and hear.

2. *How do you think your child is feeling?* Here timing for your conversation is all important. If she is upset or preoccupied, that is not the time to talk about something important. You know your child and have a sense of how she is feeling. With older children, if you are unsure, ask if this is a good time to talk. If not, tell them to let you know when it is a good time for them.

3. *What is the issue or topic and what is the message you want to convey?* Be very specific within yourself. For example, "The topic is picking up after yourself. That means picking up your toys after you play, or picking up your toys at the end of the day before bedtime. It means clearing the dining room table after you study and taking your books to your room. It means putting your book bag in your room and hanging your coat in the closet." The message is that I want you to learn to take responsibility for your belongings and respect mutual family living space. I want our home to be neat and orderly. You are an important part of this family and can do your part.

4. *What message do you want received?* Again, you cannot be too specific. Do not focus on agreement, or you will become defensive. Your message will sound controlling and invite defensiveness. Example: "I want her to hear the importance of learning self-responsibility by picking up after herself."

5. *What is the clearest way I can state my message?* Again, be very specific. Example: "I want you to grow up learning to take responsibility for yourself. One way of learning that is to get into the habit of picking up your belongings." Restate examples from #3.

6. *Ask her, "What did you hear me say?"* Wait to hear what she heard stated in her words. If there are distortions or omissions in what was heard, restate what you said. Ask again, "What did you hear me say?" Do this as often as is needed until your message is received in the way you intended. If parts are accurately received, acknowledge that part and restate the rest. For example, your twelve-year-old daughter says, "You just want me to do all the work around here." Your reply is, "No, that is not what I said. I said I want our household to run smoothly and for you to take responsibility that is yours. That means picking up your belongings. You are an important member of our family. What did you hear me say?" Keep restating what you said as often as needed until your message is heard. Stay in a calm, respectful attitude with yourself and stay with the topic. Remember, respect invites respect and respect invites cooperation.

7. *Discuss relevant details needed to develop a plan.* This may include you not reminding your child about picking up his things until the end of the day. Or it may include making sure that there is place for your child's belongings and that all family members respect each other's space. Reflect on the process. Revisit the issue from time to time and both of you assess how things are going. If you get stuck, go through the steps again. Use paraphrasing as often as you need to communicate and settle issues that usually generate conflict.

### → For Your Journal

For two weeks, pay close attention to what and how you communicate with your children. Can you be an observer of your behavior? What do you see and hear? What is respectful and what is not? If your children are old enough to copy your behavior, do you see yourself in them?

Select one part of your communication pattern that you want to change. Is it listening more closely to what you say? Is it focusing on process more than content? Is it being more patient with your timing when you need to address topics that might cause conflict? Is it paying more attention to how often you use can't, but, and why?

Write down what you want to change and create a brief plan for change. Either daily or several times a week, record your progress.

The next two weeks, select another behavior, and pay close attention. Go through the same process until you feel good about your communication behaviors.

### → Remember . . .

*When my communication is respectful, that is, clear, with careful timing, and paraphrasing, I spend more time in the short run and less time in the long run conveying my message. My words and behavior have impact and influence that cannot be retracted.*

**Chapter 6 Overview**

**Discipline: Teaching Self-Control While Avoiding Punishment and Power Struggles**

- Discipline and Punishment are Opposites
- The Purpose and Goal of Discipline is to Teach Children Self-Control
- Parents Set the Fence and Hold the Gate
- Know What the Lesson is to be Taught and Learned
- Steps for Setting and Maintaining Clear Limits
- A Behavioral Paradox: Sometimes Behavior Invites the Opposite of What the Person is Needing
- Discipline is a Gift to Your Child or a Burden on You
- Discipline is Hindered by:
- For Your Journal
- Remember . . .

# 6

## Discipline:
## Teaching Self-Control
## While Avoiding
## Punishment and
## Power Struggles

### Discipline:

- and punishment are opposites that frequently are confused.

- is an essential part of parenting: your main goal is to teach children self-control over their behaviors.

- that you have developed for yourself is directly related to your ease of limit-setting for your children. It is impossible to teach skills that you do not know, both intellectually and emotionally.

- centers on clear limits that are fences and gates that say *no* and *yes* to your children as they learn to say *no* and *yes* for themselves.

- involves your being a fence-setter and gatekeeper, one of your parenting sub-roles.

- teaches self-control; it is learned gradually as children experience clearly defined limits where they are physically and emotionally safe.

- includes limits that are reasonable for your child's developmental stage. Limits need to be reassessed from time to time as your children grow.

- includes using obvious and stated consequences to back-up your limits and give credibility to your word.

- includes knowing the lesson that needs to be taught and learned, an important step preceding setting a clear limit.

- the process of teaching and learning self-control, is in line with the behavioral paradox: sometimes behavior invites the opposite of what the person is needing.

- is a gift to your child or a burden for you.

## Punishment:

- feels extremely bad and usually results in feeling fearful, powerless, and diminished. This in turn gets projected onto others as devious, spiteful, disruptive, rude, violent, disruptive, and disrespectful behaviors.

- creates feelings of diminishment, fear, rage, pain, and vindictiveness.

- happens when parents are feeling frustrated, fatigued, insecure, unsure, powerless, scared, or angry.

- teaches children to be fearful, resentful, and angry. Children learn to fear and hate the parent doing the punishing.

- invites punishment.

## Discipline and Punishment Are Opposites

Discipline and punishment are opposites that frequently are confused. Discipline teaches lessons about behavior (what people do rather than who they are), such as being in charge of oneself, and realizing that your behavior affects others. However, punishment attacks the other person who ends up feeling powerless, and diminished. These feelings then get projected onto others as disrespectful behaviors. Punishment teaches fearfulness and vindictiveness. Other sets of opposites are also in effect.

Discipline takes a long time to develop, while punishment is instant. Discipline gives your child a way of taking more responsibility for his/her life; whereas, punishment takes away the chance of learning self-control. Discipline builds. Punishment tears down and destroys. Discipline happens when parents are feeling in charge of themselves. Punishment happens when parents are feeling out-of-control. Discipline takes much forethought; on the other hand, punishment comes from impulsiveness. Discipline is intellectual. Punishment is feeling. Discipline is a priceless gift from parent to child; in contrast, punishment is an injury. Discipline invites openness, closeness, and respect from others; conversely, punishment invites distance and punishment from others.

Knowing the difference between discipline and punishment empowers you to understand that the purpose and goal of discipline is to teach your children self-control.

## The Purpose and Goal of Discipline is to Teach Children Self-Control

Every aspect of parenting goes better for you when you have a clear purpose or goal in mind. This is no easy task, given the challenge of parenting. This applies to all of the topics covered in this book. A compounding factor is that even though each aspect of the parent-child relationship is distinct and can be discussed separately, there is considerable interrelatedness among topics. As you understand each part more clearly, then you understand the connection among the parts.

The interrelationship between discipline and self-esteem is a prime example of this separateness and connectedness: the higher your level of self-esteem, the higher your level of self-discipline. The more you are in control of yourself in a respectful manner, the more objective you are in setting and reinforcing clear limits for your child. As I have and will continue to emphasize in this book, all behavior is interpersonal; your relationship with yourself greatly affects your relationships with your children. Keep this in mind as you read the primary goal of discipline.

The main goal of discipline is to teach children self-control. It is not to punish or engage in power struggles. Punishment and power struggles only make children feel angry and vindictive with time spent calculating how to retaliate, rather than in learning important lessons about behaviors that develop self-control. The main lessons that children learn when they are punished or engaged in power struggles are how to avoid punishment, how to punish, and how to invite and escalate power struggles.

Children do not learn self-control when adults say, "Control yourself." It would be great if it were that easy. Self-control is learned in three different ways. First, it is learned as children copy and model adults' behaviors, a given and powerful assumption that holds true for all areas of the parent-child relationship. Second, it is learned as children are disciplined by parents/significant adults using clear, age-appropriate, respectful limits with consequences that are stated with the limits and adult follow-through of the consequences if needed. Third, it is learned as children experience the consequences of their own behavior and choose to learn new behaviors. A child who gets bitten by a gerbil will either learn to avoid gerbils or will learn to handle them in a way to avoid getting bitten.

The focus of this chapter is that children develop self-control as they experience the safety and security of boundaries (limits) that are clearly, not ambiguously, defined. When there is ambiguity, children feel confused and will act-out as a way of saying that the boundary is unclear and a guide for their behavior is lacking. Remember the ground rule: *Each time I speak, I really am saying more about myself than I am saying about you, even though I attach your name to it.* When you lose track of the fact that your child is saying what is going on inside him/her, the stage is set for a power struggle. The opportunity for teaching and learning self-control is gone.

You cannot be too clear or specific about the limits you set for your children. Concise, clear limits say yes or no to your children as they learn the inner controls of saying yes or no to themselves, a process that develops slowly and gradually, continuing for a lifetime. This is self-control and self-discipline.

Think of the different aspects of your life: finances, diet, exercise, emotions, career, physical and mental health, household, children, primary and secondary relationships, relationships with your parents or siblings, historical training that includes your beliefs and personal attitudes, religion, politics, leisure time, and life-in-general. Some areas you know that you are clearly in control; some areas you are struggling to take more charge, and some areas are totally out-of-control. Be honest with yourself about where you are with your life and level of self-control. Remember, where you are with your self-control affects how you discipline your children.

One of the many and varied roles within your main parenting role, called disciplinarian and teacher of self-control, is that of fence-setter and gate-keeper.

### Parents Set the Fence and Hold the Gate

Every parent desires that his/her child will learn to be responsible for his/her life. I hear this constantly from parents. You know that as children learn to control their behavior, their level of self-responsibility increases. However, what is less clear is how you function as a fence-setter and gate-keeper.

Your important job as fence-setter for your children to learn self-control includes putting in the stakes, putting up the fence, installing the gate, and being the gate-keeper. The type of fence you need to use is determined by your child's temperament and personality. Children with a mild, easy-going temperament need a chicken wire fence; whereas, children with a strong, determined will need a chain-link fence. Keep this picture in your mind to help you understand the process of how your children develop self-control.

Limits (fence and gate) allow children to feel safe, secure, protected, and loved. Given your child's developmental age, limits tell your child that you know what amount of freedom he/she can handle. Limits give space to children to explore, learn, and grow by providing guidelines (rules) for their behavior. It is putting your six month-old child who has just learned to crawl into the playpen when you answer the telephone. If you left her to roam freely while you responded to your call, you know what could happen. You, the adult, define the boundaries. Limits, at any age, are like a psychological playpen.

Your children grow quickly, so periodically you need to reassess if the stakes need to be moved out farther. It is better to set the stakes close and widen them than it is to start wide and bring them in closer. This might include allowing your five-year-old to bathe herself; letting your eight-year-old go to bed later on Friday nights than school nights; letting your twelve-year-old take total responsibility for his school work and any resultant consequences; or allowing your eighteen-year-old, who is a careful driver, to drive her friends to attend a concert that is several hours away from home.

As you periodically reassess the limits you set for your children, ask yourself: What is the lesson I have the opportunity of teaching that my child needs to learn that will enhance his/her taking more charge of his/her life? In this way, you step back from what is happening and objectively assess the situation. Decisions that are based on subjectivity (feelings) might change as your feelings change.

## Know What the Lesson is to be Taught and Learned

You as parents know that life is one continual lesson-learning. You continue to learn about yourself, others, and life-in-general. A prerequisite for clear and respectful limit-setting is knowing what the external rule is or needs to be that has the potential for teaching and learning valuable lessons about behavior.

These lessons compare with driving rules about traffic lights. You know the safety rules about red, yellow, and green lights. Have you ever gone through a red light and nothing happened? Have you ever gone through a red light and a crash happened? If you have experienced a crash, how do you behave now when you see a red light?

This provides another way for you to function in your sub-role as fence-setter and gate-keeper. What is the lesson that your child would benefit from learning? Here, you wear both your teacher and fence-setter hats. Since children's temperaments and learning-styles are individual, the time and manner in which learning takes place is also individual. Some children (and adults) learn from the first lesson, and others need the same lesson repeated over and over.

In terms of external rules and learning, think of your own life. How many lessons have you learned up to now about yourself and living? You know how much sleep you need, what foods to eat or not to eat, what is the importance of paying your bills and not spending beyond your means, what topics you can and cannot talk about with Uncle Howard, how you feel when you behave in appreciative or critical ways, how your respiratory system responds to pollen, or how you feel when you lose your patience with your children.

You continue to learn other difficult lessons. For example, you know how your anger affects you and does not change the other person's behavior. You know what happens when you feel pressured or over-stressed. You know if you do better completing a task early or letting it go until the last minute. You know when you chose to worry or feel guilty that the greatest energy drain is yours.

Think about how these lessons affect your self-control in those areas? As you know or learn the lesson, you gain more control. There is self-control in knowing the lesson for you even when you do not follow your own best advice. You (no one else) are in charge. There is self-control in knowing the specific steps in setting and maintaining clear limits.

## Steps For Setting and Maintaining Clear Limits

### → Step #1

Be clear in your mind about the lesson to be taught and learned and the accompanying limit. Take the time that is necessary to think it through or write it down if necessary. Following are some questions I hear parents ask; the lesson is indicated by parenthesis ( ).

- What is a reasonable bedtime for my four-year-old? Your answer is based on how much sleep you know your four-year-old needs. (I need _____ hours of sleep each night.)

- Where do I want my six-year-old to eat? Is your answer only in the kitchen at the table, or in the family room with dry snacks like popcorn and no ice cream or drinks, or at the dining room table when the family eats there for special occasions, or never in his bedroom, or always in the car. (**There are certain places where I can and cannot eat.**)

- What is a reasonable expectation for any of my children regarding help with household tasks or care of their personal items? Your five-year-old can put certain items on the table for a meal and your sixteen-year-old can set the table, prepare a meal, and clean-up. Your eight-year-old can sort and fold the laundry and your fourteen-year-old is capable of doing his laundry. Seven-year-olds can sort items to be recycled and ten-year-olds are capable of emptying the recylables into the larger bins. When your children are young, start teaching them to do simple tasks. As they get older, allow them to take more responsibility for regular household jobs. Be creative as you think of jobs that each child can do, trusting that she will learn, as she does the task, to perfect that skill. (**As an important member of my household, there are tasks that need to be done to help my household run smoothly, and I can do my part.**)

- What is a reasonable expectation regarding school, homework, lunches or lunch money, gym shoes for physical education days, instruments for music classes, or other deadlines? Ask yourself what amount of responsibility your child is capable of taking. If you are uncertain, ask your child's teacher or another parent what is reasonable. Your second-grader can remember which days she has physical education and needs her gym shoes. Your seventh-grader is capable of getting, completing, and handing in his homework assignments. Gradually, allow your children to take more control over their school day. (**My school work/day is my responsibility. The record that I create for me belongs to me and follows me.**)

- How much should I mediate and get in the middle when my ten- and twelve-year-olds are in conflict? Think about whether both children are capable of starting, escalating, and ending conflicts. Identify how each contributes to the fights. Does each instigate, set-off, and fuel fights? Does one child continually get set-up by the other? Is one child more likely to be peaceful and minding his own business and the other one more agitated, taking her agitation out on her brother? What happens when you get in the middle? (**The lesson for each child is learning to fight fair, minding his own business, taking ownership for what is going on inside her, not starting fights and/or learning how to resolve conflict. The lesson for you as parent is allowing your children to learn their own conflict-resolution skills, letting-go while trusting that they have what they need to learn to resolve conflict, and loving and respecting yourself enough to know their conflict is not yours.**)

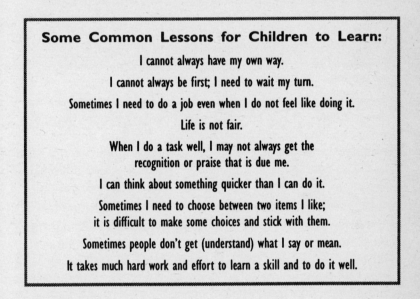

**Some Common Lessons for Children to Learn:**

I cannot always have my own way.

I cannot always be first; I need to wait my turn.

Sometimes I need to do a job even when I do not feel like doing it.

Life is not fair.

When I do a task well, I may not always get the recognition or praise that is due me.

I can think about something quicker than I can do it.

Sometimes I need to choose between two items I like; it is difficult to make some choices and stick with them.

Sometimes people don't get (understand) what I say or mean.

It takes much hard work and effort to learn a skill and to do it well.

→ **Step #2**

State clearly and specifically what your limit is starting with "I." Also state clearly the consequence if the limit is violated. Details are in Step #4. Limits can never be too clear or specific. Take time and talk with your child about the specific limit and consequence. Make sure he/she hears and understands the limit and consequence. Remember, children are so busy with their own growth and development and what is going on in their heads that your clarity is critical to helping them to hear you. Here are some examples.

- "I want you to go to bed at 7:30 and be asleep by 8:00." This is based on you knowing how much sleep your four-year-old needs and how long it takes her to wind-down and get to sleep. "I know that you do better the next day when you are rested. Your sleep is very important for you."

- "I want you to eat at the kitchen table." This is based on your knowing what happens when food is taken to other areas in the house by your four- and six-year-olds. "I know that it is easy to get distracted and have spills. If spills happen, it is easier to clean them up in the kitchen."

- "I want you to remember your gym shoes for your physical education classes." This is based on your belief that your daughter knows when her physical education classes are scheduled and can remember her shoes.

- "I want you to get, complete, and hand in your homework assignments." This is based on your belief that your 7th grader is capable of listening to, remembering, finding a time to complete, and handing in his homework assignments. It is also based on your belief that having the capability does not mean success all the time, there is room for error, and with practice, she will be successful.

- "I want both of you to learn more peaceful ways of being with each other, to talk out your differences, and at sometime in your life be good friends." This is based on your belief that each of your children has love in her heart for the other, can resolve her competition with each other, and can be good friends by the time they are adults.

- "I want you to take total charge of your laundry. This includes all of your clothes, your towels, and washable jackets. I will buy you your own laundry basket and towels and will teach you how to sort clothes, use the washer and dryer, and any other information about the care of your clothes. I will not remind you when it is time to wash your clothes." This is based on your belief that your fourteen-year-old is capable of taking this responsibility. "I know that in a few short years you will not be living at home. I am giving you the opportunity of learning to take charge of an on-going area of your life."

## → Step #3

If your child responds to your clear, specific, and direct statement, all you need to do is reinforce his/her responsible behavior. In other words, notice when your children's actions show self-responsibility and self-control. For example, you might give these responses:

- "I like the way you settled down last night and went to sleep. I love how you behave when you are rested."

- "Thank you for remembering to eat at the kitchen table. Good memory."

- "I noticed that you got all the things we need for dinner on the table. You are a wonderful helper."

- "I like the way that you are taking responsibility for your laundry. I knew you could do it."

- "It is so neat to have the wastebaskets emptied before they overflow. Thank you for being so faithful."

- "I noticed that most of the time you are remembering your gym shoes. Good for you."

- "I am so pleased with how responsible you are with your school work. I shared my good feelings about you at my meeting this morning."

- "What a peaceful way to work out your conflict. I can tell you both are growing up."

## → Step #4

For those children who are more strong-willed or preoccupied within themselves, a consequence, that is a reinforcer or back-up for your word, is necessary. Again, take time to think it through and be clear and specific. The consequence needs to be stated when you set the limit and at the first violation of the limit. Use the format: If this . . ., then this . . . will occur. Here are some examples.

- "I want you to go to bed at 7:30 and be asleep by 8:00. I know that you like me to read to you at bedtime, and I enjoy reading to you. If you are ready for bed by 7:10, that is, bathed, teeth brushed, stuffed animals arranged, then I will read to you for fifteen minutes. If you are not ready for bed by 7:10, then I will not read that night." Repeat the limit; "I want you to go to bed at 7:30 and be asleep by 8:00." The consequence is for one night only. The next night provides a chance to stay within the limits. Here is where your level of discipline affects the process.

- "I want you to eat at the kitchen table. If you do not eat at the kitchen table, then I will not serve you, or I will take your food away until you are sitting at the kitchen table." Repeat the limit. You are the adult in charge who is setting the fence and holding the gate by using a consequence. Frequently, parents are reluctant to set limits around eating for fear of depriving their children of food. However, if you follow-through with the consequence when you see it is becoming a problem, you establish a limit for your child that allows for more peacefulness at mealtime.

- "I want you to take charge of your laundry. If you do not take charge of your laundry, then you will not have clean clothes." Here, an obvious consequence follows.

- "I want you to remember your shoes on gym days. If you do not remember your shoes, I will not bring them to you. What happens then is between you and your teacher." Here, an obvious consequence is already in place.

## → Step #5

If there is a natural consequence, allow it to happen and say nothing. Your child has a chance of learning the lesson that if he does not do his laundry, he will not have clean clothes. You have already learned that lesson. Do not engage in any sermons such as, "How can you expect to have clean clothes if you do not do your laundry. You could have used the time you spent talking on the telephone or watching TV doing your laundry. Well, it isn't my problem. I guess you will have to suffer the consequence. It is all your own doing." Instead, save your breath and energy and let the obvious consequence teach a valuable lesson—the most long-lasting. Sermons invite power struggles and battles to see who is in control.

→ **Step #6**

If you stated a consequence, give one warning, then follow through the first time your child does not keep the limit. Your consequence, that is well-thought-out and reasonable, backs-up your word and limit. If you state the consequence and do not follow through, your threat and your word have no credibility. Your threatening becomes a hole in the fence for your child to slip through. Children seem to find enough fence holes themselves without your providing holes for them. Children are very direct with me about knowing which parent means what he/she says and which parent will follow through. They both respect and can count on you when you are clear with a reasonable consequence and follow-through. Otherwise, the natural consequence for your child is not learning self-control. All this relates to the following behavioral paradox.

## A Behavioral Paradox: Sometimes Behavior Invites the Opposite of What the Person is Needing

Most behavior develops and is maintained interpersonally. Children learn about themselves and their world in interactions with adults and peers. The child-adult relationship has greater impact on the child's development when children are young; whereas, the child-child (peer) relationship increases in significance as children grow to the teen years. In this way, children find their place with their generation.

A predictable paradox is that when children (and adults) are out-of-control, angry, or scared, their behavior does not invite from others what they need. In fact, their behavior invites the opposite. For instance, your daughter Ashley anticipates that she will receive an award at the end-of-the year-school assembly and feels deeply disappointed when her name is not called. When Ashley comes home, she screams at her sister and brother without their provocation. Her behavior is out-of-control, and her feelings of disappointment are hidden. Her sister and brother scream back each time Ashley screams at them. Screams invite screams. What Ashley is needing is understanding and comfort for her feelings of disappointment, not more pain and distance. If she listens to empathy about her disappointment, she can heal the wound and gain control over her emotions. If she rejects understanding, the real feelings stay hidden, get projected onto others, and invite the same behavior from others.

Children who have been accustomed to high levels of attention continue to behave in ways that invite the same level of attentiveness from others, adults and peers, long after the attention is not needed for them to function. Children with strong-willed and determined personalities carry this to extreme. They demand attention because they have become accustomed to it even though the attention might not always be best for them.

This concept, the interpersonal effect of behavior—especially what a particular behavior invites, is true about discipline, limit-setting, and the development of self-control. The times and situations when your child needs to learn self-control are the times when his/her actions are most out-of-control. This out-of-control behavior elicits anger, defensiveness, and impulsiveness; what your child needs is calmness, openness, and responses that come from rational thinking.

Giving an opposite response from what the behavior is inviting is not easy and can only come from you parents when your level of self-discipline is high and when you view your role as fence-setter and gate-keeper as a priceless gift that you give to your children. As in all other areas of parenting, your attitude toward yourself and how you view your role, affects your relationship with your children.

### Discipline is a Gift to Your Child or a Burden on You

How you view your sub-role of disciplinarian influences what you say and do. Do you view setting limits for your child as a wonderful gift or as an aspect of parenting that you hate? Is your gift a skill your child will value more and more as he/she grows? Is your duty one that you resent, avoid, or is it determined by how you are feeling at a given time? Only you can decide.

Recently, a perplexed seven-year-old told me that last Wednesday he ate a bowl of cereal in the living room, and his mother said nothing. On Friday he did the exact same thing, and his mother yelled at him. The rule or limit was unclear; he had no guide for his behavior.

The following statements can help you to identify what gets in the way as you work to give your children clear limits to enhance their self-control skills. Teaching and learning self-control are mainly interpersonal.

## Discipline is Hindered by:

- how you remember being disciplined as a child, which defines, limits, and restricts you to that experience. The challenge is for you to go beyond your experience if you were not disciplined with clear limits and respect.

- your frustration. Cool down or the frustration will be heard above anything else. No lessons are learned when frustration is primary; only fear and rage are felt. Frustration invites frustration.

- your being unclear about what the lesson is that needs to be taught and learned.

- your level of self-control, both your behavior and what you say.

- your need to punish or be vindictive.

- your children's testing the limits. Expect it from birth to age twenty-five. It goes with being a child. It is the way children check out whether you mean what you say. If you are ambivalent, they hear the wishy-washy attitude and test it, not the content of your limit.

- your lagging behind in what your children are capable of doing. Reassess where your children are developmentally. They grow fast.

- your threatening which muddies the water, undermining clear limits, and says to children, "I do not mean what I am saying and I am frustrated." If that is the case, at least be honest and save some emotional turmoil and hurt feelings.

→ **For Your Journal**

Label a section of your journal, dividing it into two sections, "My Discipline" and "My Role as Fence-setter." In the first section, identify the areas of your life where you feel good about your level of self-control. Then identify the areas that you are working on, wanting to develop more self-control, and the areas that are out-of-control for you. Remember to describe, not judge. Write down how you are doing and feeling in each area. Keep in mind the relationship between your level of self-control and your modeling and the opportunity that provides for your child to develop self-control.

In your second section, reflect on your role as fence-setter and gate-keeper. How are you doing in the job? Is there a time of day or situation that is chaotic where you can use the six steps? If so, write down how you can take your situation and make changes that are more peaceful for all. Make daily or regular entries of how the process is going. Refer to the text as often as needed. Each time you affect even a small amount of change, give yourself credit. Take time to think about both your self-discipline and your child's.

→ **Remember . . .**

- Taking the time to understand the difference between discipline and punishment empowers you to use the best teaching tools with your children.

- When you are out-of-control is not a good time to discipline your children.

- When you are in-control you are more effective with your kids.

- Children need external controls to learn internal controls.

- You and your children cannot have too much self-control.

- Clear limits make children feel safe.

- Self-control and self-responsibility are the same.

- Consequences are a wonderful back-up for what you say; use them immediately, save time, and boost respect for both you and your kids.

- Sometimes your children need something different from what they are asking. Do not always respond to their behavior at face value.

**Chapter 7 Overview**

**Power Struggles:
A Costly Battle With No Winners**

- Does This Sound Familiar?
- Understanding the Power Struggle Cycle
- Temporary and On-Going Power Struggles
- Breaking the Power Struggle Cycle
- Is Your Behavior Inviting the Opposite of What You Want?
- For Your Journal
- Remember . . .

# 7

# Power Struggles:
# A Costly Battle
# With No Winners

## Power Struggles:

- involve two family members and can last for a short time or for generations. There are no winners, only emotional scars that take much time to heal. The emotional cost is great.

- have a definite cycle of their own. Understanding the cycle allows you the opportunity to stay out of or get out of the cycle.

- occur in an emotional battleground.

- occur when one or both persons are feeling insecure, diminished, unappreciated, invisible, scared, powerless, anxious, angry, or out-of-control. Participants have lost control of themselves and believe that by overpowering the other, each can regain control. The opposite is true. When self-control is present, there is no need to control someone else.

- are sure to continue when there is debate about who started them or when the content (the topic in the struggle) is primary to the process (the struggle itself). Ending power struggles involves the decision to stop the struggle with emphasis on the process. In other words, it does not matter who starts it; it matters who ends the struggle.

- (struggling) never resolves differences or conflict.

- intensify feelings of frustration, hurt, anger, bitterness, and powerlessness resulting in a desire by the participants to be revengeful or vindictive.

- destroy trust and self-esteem.

- foster intense competition, aggression, distance, anger, and rage.

- are noted for their absence of listening, respect, and love.

- support same behaviors inviting same behaviors. Attack invites attack. Defensiveness invites defensiveness.

- are decreased when participants use "I" rather than "You" when talking to each other. "I" means more ownership for what is being said, and "You" is a way of attacking, projecting, and inviting defensiveness.

- are decreased by parents who believe they can operate outside the emotional battleground.

## Does This Sound Familiar?

The following scenarios, shared with me by parents and children, are typical examples of power struggles. Remember, none of them are bad people; they are all wonderful people. This is what happens between a parent and child when either one is feeling powerless; each struggles for power and control. The steps in the interpersonal process are identified and explained after the examples. Do any of them sound familiar?

### Scott

Two-year-old Scott's parents admit that Scott inherited each of their stubbornness and strong-willed determination which continually presents challenges to their parenting skills and drains their physical energies. By contrast, Scott's six-year-old sister Emily is easy-going, relaxed, and agreeable. (It is easier for you when your first parenting experience is with a strong-willed child. You learn about parenting, thinking this is how it is, until your second born arrives with a more calm, tranquil temperament. The contrast allows you to feel more relaxed and peaceful. Of course, since you have no control over the birth order and your child's temperament, you learn to accept what is your parenting challenge.)

At first, it was cute when Scott awoke at 4:00 a.m., crawled out of his crib, dumped the tinker toys on the playroom floor, and built a "windmill" which he enthusiastically shared as his wake-up greeting with his parents. How could they be upset with his genius and creativity? It did not take long to answer that question when his 4:00 a.m. waking became a daily routine.

At that point, both parents had more questions than answers. Does he know better? He is only two. Is this a different aspect of parenthood that they had not experienced with Emily? How do parents handle this situation in order not to stifle his creativity and independence? Is this a phase Scott is going through? If so, how long might it last? Was it something they were doing? Is this a power struggle?

The pattern continued for three months with both parents getting more and more exhausted, frustrated, and annoyed. They did everything: putting Scott to bed later in the evening, hoping he would sleep later; taking turns going to bed early as the designated one to be awakened at Scott's rising hour; sleeping in separate rooms, thinking Scott would awaken only one of them; not using the small hall light, thinking that might be the culprit; and taking Scott to his pediatrician, thinking something was wrong with him. (When you are uncertain, it is best to rule out any physical problems that might affect sleep and behavior.) To their dismay, none of their ideas or actions changed Scott's behavior.

As I listened carefully to their questions, sensing their frustration and fatigue, I asked them, "Who is in charge of the situation? Does that person have the maturity to be in charge of the situation?"

Each parent became aware that Scott definitely was in charge of his and the family's schedule. As his parents thought more, each identified other areas of Scott's growth and care where he was in charge. Then, it was clear that Scott did not have the maturity to be entrusted with responsibility for his care.

As we continued to talk and reflect, the power struggle became apparent. When you are caught in a power struggle, it is often difficult to know it at the time. Scott was in control of his and his parents' wake-up time, and his parents were feeling powerless, scared, and exhausted. Scott sensed his parents' feelings of power-lessness and took full advantage of the situation. He knew that someone needed to be in control. Young children can sense how their parents and other adults are feeling, even though adults think they are hiding their feelings. The more children sense that parents are not in control of the situation, the more vigilant children become—hence Scott's early waking hour.

The greater the level of strong-will and determination in the child, the greater the degree of control the child takes. Once the child has control of the situation, unless parents take the control that is rightfully theirs, the child gets comfortable being in charge and the behavior continues in a habitual pattern.

Scott's parents were at a disadvantage since they had no experience parenting a strong-willed child. Scott was being himself. How could they get in control without disregarding his emerging autonomy? Very simply, it meant that they needed to know that Scott was too young to define and take charge of his needs. Scott was counting on his parents to be in charge. As his parents understood what was happening, they developed an attitude of inner powerfulness, conveying to Scott that he could count on them to know what he needed. Reluctantly, Scott let go of the job that was too big for him—being vigilant. His sleep hours increased and his waking time extended to 7:00 a.m. Needless to say, the household was more balanced and peaceful with all family members getting their required sleep.

### Amanda

For Amanda, age ten, and her mother, a single mom, the battleground was predictably mornings. Mother promised herself each night that she would not battle with Amanda tomorrow morning, and each morning she broke her promise. The content of the battle varied from getting up, breakfast food, clothes, rides to school, cleaning the catbox, or turning off lights. Every morning Amanda and her mother left the house feeling angry and emotionally upset. Each of them felt miserable and edgy during her day. Neither talked about her feelings, yet both acted out what was going on inside of each of them.

At the evening meal, while feeling tense and apologetic about the morning battle, each of them attempted to be conversive and pleasant. It was difficult, at best, to cover-up the fall-out that each felt so deeply from their morning interactions. Amanda thought it was all mother's fault, and mother thought it was all Amanda's fault. Blame was the main form of connection between them. Yet, at another level of sensitivity within, each knew she had some part in the struggle, although emotions clouded their clarity of thought. Each of them was battling for control and power over the situation: who picked the breakfast cereal, who borrowed or returned whose hairbrush or belt, who got ready first or last, whose turn it was to clean the catbox, or who forgot to turn off the porch light last night.

As the three of us talked, it was difficult for Amanda and her mother to let go of blame that had been their connection for so long. There is a sense of power in what has been familiar. The blame kept the battle going and concealed the love in their hearts for each other. The content (cereal, hairbrush, catbox, lights) was secondary to the battling. What they fought about only kept the battle going.

As Amanda and her mother struggled to picture in their heads that their relationship could be more peaceful and respectful, the power struggles gradually decreased. Each learned to take increased control of herself. Mother was able to admit that at times she was behaving like a ten-year-old, rather than an adult, and Amanda admitted that she fueled the battle constantly with her strong will. Both wanted to let the love in their hearts come through to each other, rather than battle.

**Katie**

Four-year-old Katie brought her crayons and coloring book to the work table in the family room. She opened her book to a page with a picture of frogs and pond lilies. Mother admired the page as Katie selected her favorite crayon and began to color the frog purple. Mother cleared her throat, as if to say, something is wrong here. Then mother, thinking that she was using her best tack said, "Don't you want to color the frog green?" Katie replied, "No, I don't. I want to color it purple." Wonderful four-year-old independence!

The power struggle began when Mother did not let the conversation end there and began to lecture Katie about how frogs are green and not purple. This was no time for teaching about the color of water creatures. Katie knew that and responded quietly to mother by closing her book and crayon box, going off to play with her trucks, and feeling totally diminished and over-powered. The scene was another power struggle, a bid for who is going to be in control. Katie was content to pick her favorite crayon to color the picture she had selected. Katie was in charge of what she needed at that time. Her mother had another agenda. Neither was bad— just a clash of what each needed to do at a given time.

## Faye

Faye felt inadequate and embarrassed that her two-year-old Rob was the only child in the weekly play group who was not toilet-trained. Other mothers in the group flaunted how their kids had been day and night-trained for many months. Faye clearly remembered the particular Wednesday after play group when she determined in her mind that she was going to toilet-train Rob.

Faye set a schedule for Rob to sit on the toilet. She filled a big basket with toys and books. She reasoned that by keeping the basket in the bathroom, toilet training would be fun for him. The most fun part for Rob was adding toys from his playchest in his bedroom to the basket. Mother was sure that her plan was foolproof as she added a rewards-component to the schedule. There was no way that the plan could fail.

At the scheduled time, according to the plan, Faye put Rob on the toilet, allowed him to select a toy or book from the basket, and when he eliminated in the toilet, gave him a reward. At first, the plan worked. Faye felt elated and adequate. Now she had wonderful news to share with the other mothers in Rob's play group.

As the novelty of the goody basket and rewards wore off, Rob complied with mother's schedule by sitting on the toilet and refusing to eliminate. Mother, thinking maybe he did not have to eliminate, put on his training pants. Within the next half hour Rob announced to her that he was wet. Mother, thinking her timing was off, then changed the schedule from every ninety minutes to every forty-five minutes. The same pattern continued. Mother was running around frantically and Rob was being himself.

Since children learn to control their elimination process, Rob continued to tell his mother, with his behavior, that he was not ready for toilet training. Force only made Faye feel frustrated.

The power struggle continued for several months until Faye, feeling more frustrated and inadequate, realized that she wanted her son toilet-trained for her. She was able to share with mothers in the play group that she realized that she had personalized the success of the other children's toileting, believing that she was an inadequate mother. Her honesty allowed other mothers to respond with support and understanding, assuring each other that children have their own readiness timetable.

Faye was taking control of part of Rob's life that only Rob could learn to control. As she got out of the battleground, Rob trained himself and his mother.

## Maryjo

Maryjo took pride in keeping a neat, clean, and orderly home. She copied and learned this behavior from her mother who copied and learned the same from her mother. When her daughter Susie was young, Susie kept her bedroom clean, neat, and orderly to please her mother, Maryjo. There was no struggle. Mother was in control of both of them; Susie was dependent on her mother.

When Susie turned fourteen and entered high school, other activities vied for her time. She had band practice before school, soccer practice after school, horse shows to prepare for, and work at a local children's museum. In addition, Susie enjoyed helping her grandmother with household tasks.

Maryjo continued to believe that Susie needed to keep her bedroom in the same meticulous way that she had when she was a younger child. For Susie, that behavior as a younger child was no longer at the top of her list. She was not so dependent on her mother for approval and was more dependent on herself. There were mornings when she threw the covers over her bed so she would not be late for band practice. At times, she needed a few minutes in the morning to review for an exam. When weekdays were rushed, she found time on the weekends to clean her room.

This was true until Maryjo started nagging Susie daily about her room. Then the power struggle began. The only way that Susie could get back at her mother was to do the opposite, even though that went against what was important to Susie. The more Maryjo nagged, the less Susie did to keep her room clean Susie's chosen way of being in control. Her bedroom was a battleground. Susie would say, "Stay out," and her mother would go in. Susie would say, "Leave my things alone," and her mother would arrange her things. Each was struggling for control over Susie's room.

When her mother reluctantly agreed to let Susie take care of her room in her own way, the power struggle ended. Susie, feeling the control that was hers, then kept her room clean and picked up even if that happened only on weekends. It did get done, and Susie was in charge of herself. Looking back, mother realized how over-powering and controlling her behavior had been. As mother chose to have her own way, which engaged both of them in a power struggle, mother's own behavior invited the opposite of what she really wanted, a peaceful relationship with her daughter.

Children develop self-responsibility as parents let go and allow them the freedom to take control of areas of their lives that they are capable of doing. Two people cannot drive the same car at the same time. When that happens, both are headed for a collision.

The letting-go process and assessing what children are capable of doing at different ages are assets in understanding and changing the power struggle cycle. Power struggles, like other habits, have a definite pattern and cycle. As each participant understands his/her part in the cycle, changes can be made that decrease the number and intensity of the struggles.

## Understanding the Power Struggle Cycle

There is a definite pattern and cycle in power struggles. There are always two participants; the process is interpersonal. The setting is an emotional battleground. Neither person's emotions are bad; however, if the struggling continues, labels of badness get put on each other. All these labels do is reinforce each other's feelings of powerlessness, guaranteeing that the power struggle will continue. Labels limit, define, blame, judge, and keep the person who is doing the labeling from looking at what is going on inside of him/herself; labels perpetuate power struggles.

As you read in the following paragraph the four steps in power struggles, keep in mind two distinctions. First, know that you and your children are good and wonderful people; how you behave and what you do are separate from who you are. You can feel and show angry feelings without being an angry person. You can forget something without being a forgetful person. Second, know the difference between judging and describing; judging attacks the person and describing focuses on behavior. (See Chapter 2, "Describe Rather Than Judge.")

Remember to differentiate between the person and behavior; describing, not judging, fosters greater respect and peacefulness, thereby, decreasing power struggles.

First, power struggles start when you as parents are feeling powerless, inadequate, unsure, insecure, perplexed, scared, or exhausted, in general, out-of-control of yourselves or the situation. Central to the struggle or situation is what is going on inside you. It is likely, given the nature of feelings, that you are not aware of your feelings at that moment. When you are aware of your feelings, the potential for a power struggle is greatly decreased. You have more control over what is conscious for you than what is not conscious for you; yet both impact on what you do.

You as parents, the most important adults in your children's lives, behave in ways that affect your children and model behavior that your children copy. This does not abdicate children from learning to take responsibility for what they do or how they contribute to power struggles. It is important for children to learn what part belongs to them; learning that takes many years to develop. I know adults who struggle to learn this degree of self-responsibility. It follows that as you are responsible for what is going inside you, your behavior models the same.

Secondly, your feelings of powerlessness threaten a basic need in your children. Children need to know that you, the parent/adult, are in charge of yourself and the situation in order to feel secure and protected. As children feel secure and protected, these feelings become part of themselves; what follows is increased self-responsibility. Children feel insecure and unprotected when this does not happen. Knowing that someone needs to be in charge, children take control without having the maturity or skills to handle themselves or the situation.

The struggle, then, is for power or control within and over the situation; feelings of powerlessness follow a loss of inner control. When power struggles happen frequently, children grow to adulthood feeling powerless, helpless, and inadequate; the stage is set for an intergenerational struggle.

Third, your feelings of powerlessness effect how you behave and these feelings usually get projected onto your children as behaviors that are bossy, controlling, manipulative, disrespectful, rude, and intrusive. Did you ever think of these behaviors coming from feelings of powerlessness? If not, reflect on how you behave when you are feeling peaceful, calm, relaxed, and comfortable. Remember, power struggles are interpersonal. They start with what is going on inside you and affect your children. Think of it in reverse. You know the difference in your child's behavior when he/she is hungry or tired as opposed to fed and rested. the impact on you, the interpersonal effect, is also obvious.

Fourth, your child's response to feeling overpowered, controlled, and manipulated (as opposed to guided, supported, taught, and respected) is then resistance, defensiveness, and vindictiveness. Your child spends time figuring out how to oppose you, be spiteful, or defensive. The power struggle is in full swing; you each feel powerless and out-of-control. The cycle repeats unless one of you stops the battle. For young children, who are powerless and dependent, the main responsibility to stop the cycle is yours, the parent. As children grow, sensing more independence, the option is theirs to stop battling.

It is not an easy choice for children to be more mature and self-controlled than their parents. I have seen teenagers, who are tired of the painful and debilitating battles, confront their parents in loving and respectful ways and beg for the battles to stop. I applaud these teens for their courage and clear thinking. Bossy, controlling, intrusive, manipulative, rude, disruptive, and disrespectful behaviors invite bossy, controlling, intrusive, manipulative, rude, disruptive, and disrespectful behaviors. Same behaviors invite same responses. The cycle looks like this.

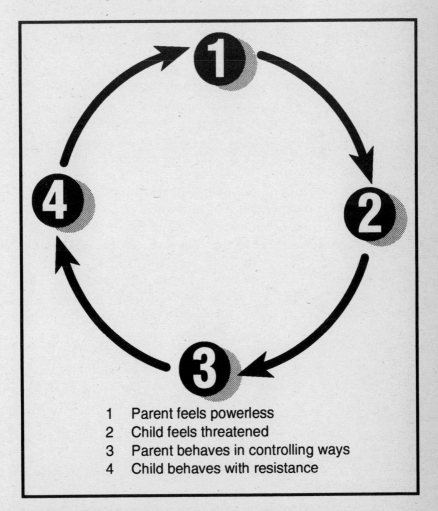

1   Parent feels powerless
2   Child feels threatened
3   Parent behaves in controlling ways
4   Child behaves with resistance

When you lose sight of what is going on inside of you and, instead, believe that the source of the struggle is your child's behavior, you behave in more controlling ways in an attempt to feel more in control; all this intensifies and compounds the struggle.

The irony is that the degree to which you are unaware of being out-of-control of yourself (internal) is the degree to which you attempt to control your external world. This is not an easy idea to grasp or believe. Yet, this concept affects power struggles that last for a short or long time.

## Temporary and On-Going Power Struggles

Some power struggles are short-lived and quickly resolved while others are on-going, lasting for generations. In both, either parent or child has lost a sense of self and his/her self-control. The temporary ones vary from a few moments or days to several months. Resolution occurs as changes happen in one or both participants. The example of Scott was related to the specifics of his strong will, his parent's lack of skill in parenting a determined, spirited child, and Scott's developmental task of sensing his first psychological separation and independence from his mother. He was declaring his independence in his typical strong-willed manner. The power struggle continued for several months until his parents understood these three factors. Then, there was resolution.

In the example of Faye and Rob, a power struggle might have been averted if Faye had not been with the other mothers in the play group comparing notes about their children's toilet-training progress. The power struggle was created when Faye interpreted the other mothers' joy of their children being toilet-trained as a statement of Faye's inadequacy. None of that was about Faye.

*Each time I speak, I really am saying more about myself than I am saying about you, even though I attach your name to it.* She heard other mothers say, "I am pleased with my child's toilet-training" and concluded, "I am a failure." In other words, she personalized their comments and felt like an inadequate mother which prompted her need to force Rob into toilet training; a power struggle was created. Feelings of inadequacy feel the same as feelings of powerlessness.

In the example of Katie, the interaction looked innocent enough when her mother wanted Katie to select the "correct" crayon color after Katie had made her selection. However, one way that Katie felt good about being in control and feeling powerful was to pick a color and better than that, to select her favorite color. Katie was saying with her behavior that I am getting so grown-up, look what I can do: I can find a page to color, I know my colors, I chose the color I like best, and I know the meaning of the word *best.* With my wonderful four year-old independence, I can do this all by myself. Wow, I am BIG! And mother, does it really matter if a four-year-old colors a frog purple?

Katie was hoping that her mother would understand that Katie was feeling so proud of what she had learned to master in four short years and would not feel threatened by Katie being a typical four-year-old.

Another example of a short-lived struggle is when you are awake most of the night responding to your sick child and your energy, patience, and tolerance for usual kid-behavior is low the next day. This kind of struggle is resolved as your child recovers and both of you get adequate rest. Other typical times are when you are dealing with external stressors like job cut-backs which threaten the family's financial security, or a serious illness of a close relative or friend. All of these times create and intensify excess fatigue or stress for both of you. The power struggle subsides when there is resolution of the situation. The long-term impact of the temporary struggles on both of you as parent and child is less than the impact of the struggles that are routine, on-going, and predictable.

The routine, predictable, and on-going struggles happen at regular times like mealtime, bedtime, morning time, as in the case of Amanda and her mother, when you are getting ready to go somewhere, when guests are coming, or more specifically when grandma comes for a visit. It is as though the specific time, based on past experience, sets the stage and becomes the stimulus that announces a battle is about to begin. In actuality, it is the feelings that you or your child bring to the occasion that get played out over and over in a predictable way. When routine power struggles are not stopped, they can go on and on, continuing for generations.

Struggling is the primary way of relating to each other and neither parent or child knows what each is battling for. Sadly, it is a way of life. Children, who are so keenly aware of the tension between their father and grandmother, say to me, "Why don't they just stop fighting and make up with each other."

A nine-year-old girl said to me, "My dad is so mean to my grandmother, his mother. Usually, they don't talk to each other at all. I don't know why they are enemies. I am so afraid that my grandmother will die because she is getting old, and they will never make up. I get caught in the middle. It feels like my dad wants me to hate my grandmother, and my grandmother wants me to hate my dad. I love each of them. I don't know what I can do. If I talk to either of them about it, they get mad at me."

The struggle is so primary that neither of you can remember how the battle started or what each of you are battling for or about. Each of you believes that it is the other person's behavior that caused or keeps the battle going. The truth is the battle is more about what is going on inside each of you; that is all that you control. *I am responsible for and to myself and I create my own experiences and feelings.*

The example of Maryjo and Susie had the potential of becoming an on-going and generational struggle given Maryjo's need (learned from her mother and not good or bad) for a clean, tidy house. Fortunately, when Maryjo realized the importance of letting go of her need to be in charge of Susie's room, the struggle ended. Susie's need for independence, to take charge of her room, was of greater importance for her than mother's need (to be in control of) a clean house. Maryjo gave Susie a priceless gift of changing, rather than repeating history. The new, learned behaviors will continue to be taught and learned through the coming generations. The obvious question for you that follows now is what are some more ways of ending a power struggle?

## Breaking the Power Struggle Cycle

Breaking the cycle is easier in the short-lived power struggles than in the on-going ones. In the example of the sick child, as soon as the parent is rested, regains his/her energy, feels in charge of himself and the situation, the child feels secure and protected. The power struggle ends. It is clear that the parent then is in charge.

In the on-going power struggles, the task is more difficult and challenging, yet possible, since the interpersonal pattern is well-ingrained and habitual. Just like the power struggle cycle, there are definite steps to follow to break the pattern.

First, you as parents need to picture in your thinking how the scenarios can be different. After it is evident that there is a power struggle, the following is a common dialogue between parents and me.

Counselor: Can you see or imagine a different scene, interacting with your child in another way? I hear how it is now. How would you like for it to be?

Parent: I know it will never change. It happens every morning. I am at the point where I hate mornings.

Counselor: I hear how it is now, so painful and stressful. It is difficult to begin to imagine another way. Your thoughts of how it is now reinforce the pattern that has become so familiar and make change impossible. You control your thinking and it is powerful. Only as you picture a peaceful morning can you begin to make changes. Yes, it is difficult to think in ways different from how situations have been. That picture in your head is very clear. It means stretching your imagination; your mind is capable of changes.

Parent: So if I picture in my head not fighting with Amanda each morning and being pleasant and relaxed, it can come true?

Counselor: Yes, you will be more aware of what is happening inside you than of what Amanda is doing. Every little change you make, each time you control yourself, contributes to lessening the intensity and frequency of the power struggles. The process occurs gradually.

Second, it is knowing that it is not your child's behavior that causes or continues power struggles. It is what is going on inside you: your beliefs, attitudes, feelings, your perception of your child's behavior, your reactions to your child's behavior, and your conclusions that you draw about your child and yourself from your child's behavior. In the true sense, since you and your child are two separate people, you have no control over your child's behavior. You can model, teach, guide, reinforce, remind, and even punish. You cannot make your child think, feel, or behave in certain ways. This applies to any age child.

Continuing to focus on your child's behavior, rather than the person you have control over—you, is easier. Next is continuing the power struggle.

Third, identify what modifications are necessary for you to make in your behavior that will get you out of the emotional battleground. What modifications are you willing to make? How can you make the non-power struggle picture in your head come true? How can you adopt the belief that the conflict between you and your child is not coming from your child's behavior? How can you remember that same behaviors invite same responses? The following questions can help you to make modifications in your behavior that are more self-respecting. As these concepts make sense to you, create your own approach or technique to make your desired change. You have all of the resources within you that you need.

- Can you believe that your relationship with your child is too short and precious for you to be battling frequently?

- Can you believe that you both deserve more peacefulness and respect?

- Can you tolerate fewer battles and create more peacefulness?

- Can you see yourself as the adult whose behavior has much impact?

- Can you switch to using "I" rather than "you" which communicates greater ownership for what you are saying? "You" defines, attacks and invites power struggles.

- Can you respect and love yourself enough to look at what your behavior is modeling for your children?

- Can you believe that loving yourself is the greatest gift you give to your children?

- Can you take an honest look at what your behavior is inviting?

## Is Your Behavior Inviting the Opposite of What You Want?

As stated in Chapter Six "On Discipline," this is an on-going question in all areas of parenting. Another way of dealing with power struggles is by asking yourself the question: Is my behavior inviting the opposite of what I want? You and what you do are important and powerful. Many of your behaviors developed as you were growing up and are part of how you view yourself. They are so much a part of you that you take your behaviors for granted, let alone, critique them from time to time. I frequently hear parents say that they want different behaviors from their children, yet fail to examine their own behaviors. You are too important to bypass yourself.

### → For Your Journal

Reflect on the times and situations when you engage in power struggles with your children. Think of the four steps in the power struggle. Do you battle with one child more than another? What sense do you make of that? Is that particular child most or least like you? When do the struggles happen: mornings, bedtime, mealtimes, when you are getting ready to go somewhere or are preparing for guests? How do they start? What keeps them going? Who starts them and who ends them? Do any of them get resolved? What is the content? What are the underlying issues?

Note what is going on in you: how you feel, what your expectations are, and what you say and do. Look carefully at what the steps are that lead to and continue the struggle. Slow down the process as though you are viewing the interactions through a powerful microscope. Record each step. Only as you identify each step can you make changes that bring respect and peacefulness to your relationships with your children.

As you identify your part of and contribution to the power struggle, share your awareness with your children. What a wonderful way to model openness, honesty, and humanness. What a wonderful way to decrease the fighting and tension. What a wonderful way to create more respect and peacefulness.

→ **Remember . . .**

- Each person in a power struggle contributes in some way; it can be active or passive.

- Children and parents with strong wills have a harder time getting out of power struggles. Each wants to have the last word.

- Your children sense when you are giving them permission to take charge of certain tasks.

- Two people cannot drive the same car at the same time.

- To let go of your control over your children involves knowing what kids are capable of doing at different developmental stages.

- Labels fuel power struggles.

- Power struggles are destructive to all participants.

- You as parents can never feel too secure, respectful, and peaceful within yourselves.

**Chapter 8 Overview**

**Conflict in the Child-Child Relationship:
What is Your Role?**

- Rivalry Among Siblings is Part of Growing Up
- Sibling Rivalry: An Arena to Learn Conflict Resolution
- Teaching Lessons of Respect and Personal Boundaries
- Your Need for Harmony and Control Intensifies Sibling Rivalry
- Your Fear Reinforces the Behavior You Dislike
- Your Response to Sibling Rivalry
- For Your Journal
- Remember . . .

# 8

# Conflict in the Child-Child Relationship: What is Your Role?

### Sibling rivalry:

- is as old as Cain and Abel. When there are two or more children in the family, there will be differences and conflict. Rivalry among siblings is part of growing up.

- between your children activates your unresolved historical issues with your own siblings; unresolved past issues affect your perceptions of and reactions to what you see happening between your children.

- grants an arena for brothers and sisters to learn how to deal with conflict. For you parents, it is an opportunity to teach peaceful resolution skills.

- allows you to teach your children primary lessons about the processes of respect (regard, esteem) and personal boundaries (ownership of issue).

- has a goal, among many, of getting attention and reactions from you. Strangely enough, it is a way of connecting with you.

- is intensified by your need for harmony and control; your issues compound and confuse your children's issues. Harmony grows as you and your child engage in a reciprocal letting-go process;

you let go of control and your child takes control and learns self-responsibility.

- fosters fear in you that your children's fighting, whether physical or verbal, will never end. Your fearfulness clouds your objectivity, reinforces behaviors that you do not like, and fosters more fear.

- involves blind faith for you to believe that your children, if allowed the time, will work out their conflicts with each other and will have learned valuable resolution skills. The fringe benefit for you is increased patience.

- among your children is affected by the degree to which you have learned to resolve your inner and interpersonal conflicts. In other words, your level of inner peacefulness affects your response to their conflict.

- is intensified when you take sides, which is different from understanding what is happening within and between your children in conflict.

- involves knowing that the content of the conflict is secondary to the process. At times, the reasons, needs, pay-offs, or gains are not conscious.

- includes knowing that conflict and peacefulness are opposites; both are processes that take time to learn, develop, and maintain.

## Rivalry Among Siblings is Part of Growing Up

Growing up with siblings means hand-me-downs, teasing, competition, companionship, bickering, loving, fighting, brotherhood, sisterhood, tears, and jealousy; all of these create personal identity and develop coping skills. All of these are affected by birth order, your parenting experiences and confidence, your child's personality and temperament, and you and your child's energy and frustration levels. Unless you remember how you felt about and related to your siblings, you might find yourself challenged and frustrated by your children's competitive behavior. If you were an only child who now has several children, your experience with your children's competition means learning as you go not having the bias of your childhood affect your objectivity.

Remember, in all areas of parenting, your best resource for understanding your children is your childhood. What do you remember about your relationship with your siblings? What words characterize your relationships, first as children and now as adults? How you experienced competition with your brother(s) or sister(s), including, how you felt, the way each of you competed, and your parents' roles, color your attitude and feelings toward your children's competitiveness. If you were an only child, how did you view other sibling relationships? What did you like about being an only child and what was missing for you?

Again, as a main theme in this book, you cannot bypass yourself the most important person in your child's life. As with all of life, each experience affords a lesson to be learned and taught. Sibling rivalry allows that opportunity to teach and learn peaceful conflict resolution skills. Parents frequently tell me that they feel more like frustrated referees, mediators, and arbitrators rather than teachers, role models, and mentors when it comes to their children's bickering, quarrelling, and fighting. Sibling rivalry is an important part of growing up.

## Sibling Rivalry:
## An Arena to Learn Conflict Resolution

It is difficult to see yourself as a teacher of life-skills when you are in a learner role, getting your parenting training on-the-job. To compound this, rivalry and competition have so many emotions involved that often the bigger picture and objectivity get obscured.

Competition and rivalry among siblings offer an opportunity to learn and practice conflict resolution skills in the safety of family and home. What better place to learn such valuable skills! Too often, you get upset with the effects of the constant and predictable fighting and lose track of what the lesson is to be taught by you and learned by your child. Unfortunately, without realizing it, you become part of the conflict rather than the solution.

The main lessons that children need to learn when there is conflict are respect for individual differences and the importance of personal boundaries. These are the underlying concepts from which to develop conflict resolution skills. In order to effectively teach any skill, either with your actions or talking, you must understand what ideas undergird them.

Respect and personal boundaries are essential for all relationships.

## Teaching Lessons of
## Respect and Personal Boundaries

Every time your children experience conflict between themselves, you have the opportunity to teach valuable lessons of respect and personal boundaries. I am sure that when your children start fighting the last idea that pops into your head is, "Here is a wonderful opportunity right now to teach my kids lessons of respect and personal boundaries." No doubt the first idea that comes to mind is, "Oh, no, here we go again. Will these kids ever be friends?"

Personal boundaries and respect are interrelated and interdependent. Respect cannot exist without personal boundaries and personal boundaries cannot exist without respect.

Respect focuses on the question, "How can I accept and regard you when we have differences?" Personal boundaries focus on the question, "Whose issue and/or responsibility is this?"

Personal boundaries are violated when one person behaves in ways that are abusive, hurtful, disrespectful, rude, annoying, or uncomfortable to another person. In other words, when people overstep their bounds, violating their own birthright of self-respect and invade your bounds, violating your birthright of being treated respectfully, boundaries are disrupted. What you do to another person first, affects you, and secondly has impact on the other person.

Children, dependent on adults, frequently have their personal boundaries violated; they grow to adulthood without respectful boundaries and behaviors. Children learn what they experience. Such was the case for Dillon and his sons, nine-year-old Evan and thirteen-year-old Mark.

Dillon's eyes watered as he shared that his sons were in constant turmoil. He felt that his sons hated each other and that he was a bad father. Intellectually, he knew this was not so. This is the conversation that followed.

Counselor: Do I hear you correctly that Evan and Mark are in constant conflict?

Father: Yes, it starts when they wake up and doesn't end till they fall asleep at night. It tears me apart. It is so constant. They are good kids and each is so pleasant when alone. The minute the other one walks into the room bingo, they are at it again. I yell at both of them to stop. I feel like a policeman. The only way that I can get them to stop is to send each to his room. Recently Evan is starting to say before I do, "I know, I'll go to my room." What am I doing wrong?

Counselor: You are not doing anything wrong. No judgment. Do you believe that your sons love each other?

Father: Yes, I know they do. With all the conflict, it's hard to see it.

Counselor: What exactly do they do?

Father: Well, like yesterday afternoon, Mark was reading a book in the family room. He loves to read and is a good reader. I guess you'd call him a bookworm. Then Evan came in and took Mark's bookmark off the table. Mark ignored him, so Evan threw a pillow at him. Mark still ignored him, then Evan got his water pistol and started squirting him. That did it! Mark flew out of the chair, grabbed his water pistol, and soaked Evan. Then Evan screamed, and his mother came running to settle the fight.

Counselor: So Evan heckles and teases his brother, and Mark ignores him until Mark reaches his limit?

Father: Mark ignores him for awhile, but Evan keeps on. Sometimes Mark gets so angry that he goes to his room and Evan follows. If Mark closes his door, Evan bangs on the door and won't stop. By that time, I am so mad that I am ready to throw both of them out. It might calm down for a bit, then it starts all over again. When I think about it, rarely does Mark start the fights; it is usually Evan.

Counselor: It sounds like Evan needs to learn to respect Mark's closed door and find another activity for himself. What is Evan getting when he behaves in those ways?

Father: He's getting me real mad for one thing. And he sure gets attention from his brother. Why would he want that kind of attention?

Counselor: As strange as it may sound, attention is attention and is a way of connecting with another person. Evan is getting much attention and sure is persistent with his invitation for attention. Also, it sounds like some other factors are at play; maybe we need to look deeper at what else keeps reinforcing Evan's behavior. Any behavior that children (or adults) keep using has some kind of a pay-off or gain. Often the reasons are not conscious. I want to help you figure out what keeps Evan's behavior going.

Father: I never thought about Evan getting attention and persisting, or his behaviors getting pay-offs. When they're going at it, it just feels awful.

Counselor: I can hear your frustration. I need to ask you a few questions. First, I heard you say that you think you are doing something wrong because your sons are in so much conflict. Were you ever teased when you were a kid?

Father (with tears in his eyes): My dad teased me all the time. He could never say a serious word to me. I guess you could call him a practical joker. He teased my sister too.

Counselor: Could you ever tell him how you felt?

Father: Whenever I tried, he'd make a joke out of it.

| | |
|---|---|
| Counselor: | Could you tell your mother how you felt? |
| Father: | Whenever I would talk to her, she'd say, "Oh, your father doesn't mean it. That's how he shows you that he loves you." |
| Counselor: | So, your father's only way of connecting with you was to heckle and tease. Maybe he did not know any other way to be with you. |
| Father: | I guess he didn't. His dad teased him a lot. Both of them tease my boys, especially Evan. Evan is my dad's favorite. |
| Counselor: | Does your dad love your boys? |
| Father: | I am sure he does. |
| Counselor: | Do your boys love their grandfather? |
| Father: | Oh, yes. |
| Counselor: | Has Evan ever heard you say that his grandfather teases people as a way of showing he loves them? Have you ever made that comment to another adult when Evan could have heard it? |
| Father: | Oh, I'm sure it could have happened. |
| Counselor. | So, Evan has heard you say that grandpa (and perhaps great-grandpa) teases people he loves. He has experienced his grandfather's teasing all the time and knows his grandpa loves him, and he does not know how painful teasing was for you as a child and how you hated it. Evan also knows that he loves Mark and continues, persistently, to let Mark know it. Evan gets confused when you keep telling him to stop doing something that he has learned from you and his grandfather; teasing is a way of showing others that you love them. For a nine-year-old boy, what his father, grandfather, and great grandfather, three very important males, say and do is like the gospel truth. |

| | |
|---|---|
| Father: | That is a way of looking at it that makes sense. So why does Evan want to do something that is so painful to me? |
| Counselor: | He doesn't want to hurt you. He does not know about your pain. That is your issue and your pain from your childhood; it is within your personal boundary and belongs to you. Evan loves and emulates his grandfather and is copying his behavior in addition to responding to what he has heard you say, "Grandpa teases, that is how it is, and that is his way of showing love." Both you and Mark have been on the receiving end and know how heckling and teasing feels. When personal boundaries are invaded, it hurts. |
| Father: | It sure is upsetting. I have never had a serious conversation with my dad. I don't know if I ever will. |
| Counselor: | Before you tackle your dad, would you like to see if there are some ways of decreasing the tension between Mark and Evan? |
| Father: | I sure would. |
| Counselor: | The following is an example of what you can say to Evan at a time when both of you are feeling relaxed and have time to talk. |
| | Evan, I think I understand the reason for the constant bickering that goes on between you and Mark. Some of my understanding is connected to me and my dad (your grandpa), and some is about you and Mark. |
| | I know that you have heard me say that grandpa is a big tease, and he teases the people he loves the most You learned that from me. Plus, you see grandpa teasing you all the time, and I know that you love him and he loves you. However much grandpa loved me, his teasing hurt my feelings when I was a little boy. Now, when you tease Mark and he is hurt, I am reminded of how I was hurt. So that is the reason |

I ask you to stop the teasing and go to your room.
This must be confusing to you. You are showing your
love by teasing just the way grandpa and I have
taught you. Then I contradict myself. Please forgive
me for teaching you one thing and when you do it,
telling you to stop. Since that way upsets Mark, can
you think of another way that you can show Mark
you love him? I want the teasing and bickering to stop.
It is too painful for me and Mark.

Father:    I will talk to him and see what happens.

A week later, Dillon told me that he had a serious conversation
with Evan; it was the talk that Dillon had never had with his dad.
Evan listened intently. When Dillon asked Evan how he could show
his love for Mark in another way, Evan replied, " I can be nice to
him." And that is what he did for a week until one day he slipped
back into the old pattern. At that moment, he caught himself,
looked at his dad and said, "Oops, I forgot about our talk." Evan's
behavior changed.

Two weeks passed and Dillon called me to share that Evan had
come to him last night after they had returned from a visit at his
grandfather's house and asked, "Dad, remember our talk? I don't
tease Mark anymore. Are you going to talk to grandpa too?" What
wisdom comes from children.

I knew that Dillon needed time to think about that one. Con-
fronting his father directly was a separate issue from responding
to his sons. What I chose to do was reinforce Dillon for changing
his history by teaching his sons more respectful ways of relating
and creating wholesome personal boundaries for themselves.

Dillon's boundaries were violated as a child when he was constantly teased. The teasing felt horrible, and there was no one he
could talk to who listened or took him seriously. Dillon connected
with his father in the only way his father knew. Dillon never once
questioned his father's behavior or the impact of his father's behavior; Dillon, concluded it was himself.

No adult was there to tell Dillon that both he and his dad were
good people, or that it was fine for Dillon to listen to his heart and

feel the hurt from being teased, or that his father (grandpa) was behaving from what he had learned as a child.

Instead, Dillon doubted his feelings and himself. The self-doubt carried into Dillon's fathering. Children usually doubt themselves, rather than question the adult's behavior. When children's boundaries are disrupted and violated, children do not realize that it is more about what is going on inside the adult than them. *Each time I speak, I really am saying more about myself than I am saying about you, even though I attach your name to it.* Children grow to adulthood repeating the same behaviors with their children.

It is impossible to overemphasize the importance of respectful boundaries in all relationships, especially the parent-child connection. Respect and regard are nurtured when parents are sensitive to their children's feelings and rights.

When you are not aware of the importance and processes in developing personal boundaries, you often want and demand harmony instead of examining your childhood experiences. The impact on sibling conflict intensifies, rather than decreases, the rivalry.

## Your Need For Harmony and Control Intensifies Sibling Rivalry

Parenting and growing-up demand a reciprocal letting-go. You let go of your child as he/she becomes more self-reliant, and as your child is more self-reliant, he/she lets go of you. Letting go means less dependency on you and for your child more dependency on him/herself.

This idea is more apparent to parents in areas of physical responsibility than psychological responsibility such as conflict. It is easier for you to let your children feed themselves, wash their faces and hands, and mop up the spilled milk than it is to allow them to feel their feelings and take time to learn their own wisdom in their own time and way. Why is this so difficult in practice?

The first reason is that you probably have forgotten about your own sibling clashes, and second, you want harmony now. Part of your desire for harmony makes you impatient; you demand it, which keeps you in control of the situation. All of this deprives your children of learning conflict resolution skills, or if they have them, using them in front of you.

I am reminded of a call I received from Diana, a single mother of eleven-year-old David and fourteen-year-old Glen. She was feeling distressed because her sons "are always fighting." She stated that all she does from morning to night is unsuccessfully stop fights. I later learned that this was an exaggeration, a sure way of staying in control because it sounds so extreme and serious. The process of the fighting is more primary than the content such as who picked the last TV program, whose turn it is to sit in the front seat, and who got the biggest or last cookie.

Diana gave me permission to talk with her sons about their conflicts and both came willingly. I told them that their mother was distressed about their fighting and the following conversation ensued.

| | |
|---|---|
| Counselor: | Tell me about the fights. |
| David: | Well, we do fight. |
| Counselor: | How much? |
| Glen: | Well, sometimes. |
| Counselor: | Your mother says it is all the time. How do you see it? |
| David: | Not all the time. Sometimes we are friends. |
| Counselor: | When are you friends? |
| Glen: | Mostly when we are home alone. |
| Counselor: | Do you fight when your mother is not at home. |
| Boys: | No. |
| Counselor: | I don't understand. You fight when your mother is home, and you do not fight when your mother is gone. Help me understand the difference. |
| David: | Well, we don't want to hurt each other or break stuff. |
| Glen: | Yea, we'd be responsible for what happened, and we don't want to clean up a mess. |
| Counselor: | It sounds like you are in total agreement about that. I still don't understand. You each take responsibility |

> and are in agreement with each other when your mom is gone, and you don't take responsibility when she is at home.

David:  Well, you know how adults are. Like they need to be in charge.

When I shared with Diana what I had learned from my talk with her sons, she was shocked. As she thought about it, she realized that she had a high need to be in charge. Since she was a single parent, the need seemed justified. She knew she had to let her boys take responsibility when she was there just as she had communicated that it was agreeable with her when she was not at home. She let go in two ways.

First, Diana let go of control by eliminating the numerous detailed instructions she gave when she asked her sons to do a task; details which each son knew and resented as constant reminders of her control. A common one was a prompt to put on the dog's leash every time each son walked the family pet. Both boys were well aware of the leash law and safety for their pet.

Secondly, Diana moderated her use of exaggeration words like always and never. These words do not allow or invite input from others. As Diana decreased her controlling behaviors, her sons' behaviors became more responsible and their fighting decreased considerably when she was home.

Siblings' competitiveness may have much to do with the children involved, or with you as parents, or a combination of the two. Harmony often takes considerable time, understanding, and patience to develop. Think of your relationship(s) with your siblings. Is your relationship harmonious now? Was it when you were kids? If not, what were some of the issues that you resolved or still need to resolve.

I hear some common themes from parents and children that are related to birth order and age, strengths and weaknesses, parental rules and limit-setting, personality and temperament, and development of personal identity; all decrease or increase independence and individuality. The way these themes are evident are shown in the following examples.

### Terry and Anne

Terry and Anne were born thirteen months apart. Terry had multiple medical problems which delayed her growth and development. Anne, on the other hand, was healthy and somewhat advanced in her developmental milestones. Frequently, people assumed Anne was the first-born.

Their conflict centered around Terry being the oldest in age, yet Anne constantly surpassing her in learning skills. Terry was aware of her limitations and how her sister excelled. Anne was aware of her abilities and was constantly torn between being herself and waiting for her sister to catch up. The primary conflict was between Terry and Anne. Both needed much time to grow and deal with accepting their differences. Children are very aware of their birth order.

### Jessica and Patty

Jessica and Patty were four years apart. Jessica was born with much determination and stubbornness, and there were many conflicts between her and her parents before Patty was born. Patty's temperament was easy-going; it took a lot to get her upset. Their conflict related to the extremes in their approaches to life. Jessica both admired and hated Patty's low-keyed manner. Jessica constantly overpowered Patty, wanting her to answer questions now or sooner, while Patty wanted time to think. Jessica's tone of voice was usually sharp and demanding; Patty's tone was calm and subdued.

Their conflict arose because Patty was an easier child to parent. The easier temperament invited easier parent responses and was a separate issue from love and loving. The conclusion that Jessica drew was that her parents favored Patty and loved her more which heightened Jessica's intensity. When Jessica took her frustration out on Patty, either parent would step in attempting to create harmony. Patty was responsive to her parent's intervention which only made Jessica more upset, and the cycle continued.

As of now to decrease or lessen the above conflict, both parents need to keep admitting to themselves (and each other) the extreme differences in personality and temperament of their children and accept the energy needed to respond to each of them. Children with intensity can wear you out fast. Jessica can learn to soften her voice and bossiness, as she struggles to know that she is in charge of what responses she invites from others. Patty needs to know that she can be herself, and that when she is overpowered by Jessica, it is more about what is going on inside Jessica than her. *Each time I speak, I really am saying more about myself than I am saying about you, even though I attach your name to it.* And yes, all of these are tall orders and difficult lessons for children and adults to learn.

### Jamison

The example of seventeen-year-old Jamison, an only child for ten years when his sister Laura was born, shows how sibling conflict can come from parental rules that change over time. Jamison's parents grew up with very strict rules and, therefore, were very strict with him. When Laura was born, his parents were most lenient with her; Jamison was enraged. He took his rage out on Laura who got him back by tattling. Every move Jamison made, Laura watched and told their mom and dad. Jamison hated being monitored by a seven-year-old sister. You can imagine the turmoil that created!

The turmoil decreased as Jamison's parents acknowledged that they had been harder on him and in Jamison's words, "Laura gets away with everything." His parents realized that they had changed and mellowed through the years and were more relaxed with themselves and their parenting. They were so thrilled to have a daughter after so many years that their joy made them more tranquil.

For Jamison, the change was too late for him except to understand the change and to stop being angry at his parents for changing. Before his parents were aware of how their change in parenting contributed to the rivalry, their greatest fear was that their children would always battle.

### Your Fear Reinforces the Behavior You Dislike

Conflict is stressful and scary. When you are afraid, you are filled with apprehension about what you see happening. Your fear is that there will always be conflict. Many parents share with me that they have a picture in their heads about how they want their children's relationship with each other to be. When your children's behavior is different from your picture, you draw erroneous conclusions, such as, maybe there is something wrong with you or your children, or kids should not fight. When the behavior you dislike or find stressful continues, you get more scared. Some of you may even feel angry, and I challenge you to look deeper and see that your anger is covering up fear.

Children tell me that sometimes they fight to get your reaction. It is a predictable way of getting attention; it gives children a momentary sense of satisfaction and a false sense of power to see your reaction. Wow, what I did got my dad to pay attention! For example, your daughter anticipates your reply, "Don't do that," when she torments her younger brother. When you repeatedly respond to a behavior that creates or perpetuates conflict, you actually reinforce the very behavior that you do not like. You know what happens when you hit a tent stake repeatedly; it goes deeper and deeper into the ground.

For some reason, probably habit, you keep using the same responses over and over. Habit reinforces habits. I love to hear parents share how their different responses in conflictive situations invite unfamiliar reactions. This is an option for you, or a new response to sibling rivalry. New and different self-respecting responses produce changes.

### Your Response to Sibling Rivalry

It takes patience and blind faith to believe that your children, at some point, will learn how to resolve their differences, no matter where they originate, in respectful and peaceful ways. Children have infinite potential; potential takes times to develop. Children need parents who believe in them even when their behavior is unbelievable and self-defeating.

You have read about the two main concepts underlying children's conflict, respect and personal boundaries and your need for harmony and control. Keep this bigger picture in mind as you approach and deal with the day-to-day situations that arise. Also, remember that your level of inner peacefulness affects your response to your children's conflicts. When you are feeling powerless, left-out, scared, invisible, tense, or upset, your behavior is different from when you are feeling powerful, peaceful, and secure.

Your overall goal, during sibling conflict, is to teach your children inner coping skills that allow them to develop respectful personal boundaries. Like in all other areas, your response to children under five or six needs to be different than with older children.

As your children grow, the conflicts and their ability to handle them change. Your role gradually changes from protector to impartial facilitator to observer. Use the guideline, my involvement in conflicts decreases as my children get older. Your patience with the process, as difficult as it is, is an asset that models patience and tolerance and sends a nonverbal message, "I know you can handle this situation."

Children under five or six need your protection from each other to create boundaries where each child will be physically and emotionally safe. Children over five have learned to take some responsibility for their actions and need an opportunity to learn ways of resolving their conflicts. When there is a considerable difference in age, size, or emotional intensity, your involvement is essential. When your three-year-old is hitting your eleven-month-old on the head, you need to remove one of them quickly. When they are thirteen and eleven, you will participate less in their competition.

Children six and older need time and space to resolve conflict. Parents (and other adults) are often remiss in jumping in too soon. This is the challenge of the letting-go process which includes allowing children to figure out how they got into a situation, how they stay in a situation, and how to get themselves out of a situation. For you, with your learned wisdom, the answers are easy.

Some of your answers are if only you would not: tease or challenge your sister, take issue with every word your brother speaks, jump to conclusions before you have all of the information, think you know everything, interrupt your sister, need to have the final word, agitate your brother when he is calm, be angry at what is out of your control, or be disrespectful of your sister's belongings.

Keep foremost in your thinking that your children need time to have their experiences that, with time, become their life philosophy, inner controls, and wisdom. Your task is to believe that your children can and will learn from all of their experiences to use prudence and discretion, better known as common sense. Your patience, self-acceptance, peacefulness, and self-respect enhance this process.

Patterns get established quickly where the pay-off for the quarrel is getting your attention or getting you to take sides. Ask yourself, before you jump in, if your involvement is needed for safety reasons, or if it is your need for harmony or control. If your answer is for safety reasons (someone is being overpowered or could get badly hurt) then step in and stop the fight. If your answer is more for your need for harmony and control, back out graciously, giving your children time and space to work out their differences.

Remember not to get caught up in the content or the words spoken during a conflict. The words are more an expression of the feelings at that moment which keep the conflict going. The process of the conflict is primary to the content, the spoken words. Have you ever participated in a conflict and a day or so later forgot what (the content) you were fighting about, yet you remembered the fight? Remember this especially when you are in a facilitator role in the middle of or after a conflict. Your knowledge of the difference between content and process is an asset to your objectivity; it allows you to ask questions that prompt your children to think about their roles in the conflict and keeps you from taking sides.

When you are in a facilitator role, ask the following questions to give your children the chance to think about their responsibility, choices and options.

- What do you think is going on between you and Jimmy?
- What is going on inside you? How are you feeling?
- What do you think is going on inside Angie?
- What do/did you want to see happen?
- What do you need to say to Judy? What else?
- Is there more that you need to say to Judy?

- What is the problem?

- Can the problem be solved? If yes, how can the problem be solved? If no, what is standing in the way of the problem getting solved?

- What can each of you learn from this fight? Let each child answer this question. If more time is needed, take a break and reconvene at a later time.

Like discipline and power struggles, taking more time in the short run eliminates taking more time in the long run. The lessons are more long-lasting. Take the time to talk about the conflict. Listen carefully to each child, allowing ample time for each to share his/her perceptions, feelings, reactions, and solutions.

Children need to feel accepted as people, separate from how they behave, and need time to develop and access their inner resourcefulness and creativity to learn from their differences. Your impartial facilitation helps.

Always keep the bigger picture in mind. Conflict and peacefulness are opposites. Both are processes that take time to learn, develop, and maintain. Experiencing conflict allows you to appreciate peacefulness.

### → For Your Journal

Spend some time thinking about your relationship with each of your siblings. To whom were you closest? Whom did you fight with the most? What was your parents' response to your fighting? How do you wish it would have been different? What is your relationship now with your siblings? What or who has changed? In what ways? Record what is significant to you.

Think about each of your children's relationships with each other. How do you view and describe their relationships? Are some more conflictive than others? How are their conflicts created, and how does each contribute to the strife? What does each do to keep the battle going? What is your role? Given the age of your children, has your role changed much over the past years? What is your greatest fear regarding your children's relationships with each other?

From time to time, think about these questions and make your journal entries.

→ **Remember . . .**

- If you have more than one child, there will be some degree of competition and rivalry between them.

- Your childhood and current experiences with conflict affect your role in your children's relationships.

- You give your children a valuable gift when you allow them time to learn conflict resolution skills.

- Unwittingly, you may be reinforcing behaviors that are disrespectful.

- Your children need to experience conflict before they can appreciate peacefulness.

- Words used during conflict are an expression of what is going on inside your children at that moment.

- The letting go process is another skill that you are learning on-the-job.

**Chapter 9 Overview**

**Feelings**

- Your Feelings are an Important Part of You
- You Feel Many Feelings—Either Primary or Secondary
- Your Feelings Blur Your Objectivity
- Your Feeling and Self-Esteem are Directly Related
- How You Feel Inside May be Different From How You Behave
- History is Repeated Through the Familiarity of Feeling Responses
- As a Child Did You Feel . . . ?
- You Can Accept Feelings Without Condoning the Behavior That is an Expression of the Feelings
- Feelings That are Kept Inside Build and Increase in Intensity—Feelings That are Expressed Lose Their Intensity
- You Change your Feelings by Changing Your Thinking
- For Your Journal
- Remember . . .

# 9

# Feelings

## Feelings:

- are an important aspect of your parenting and your humanness. Accept them.

- include: anxiety, apprehension, calmness, despair, depression, disappointment, dismay, doubt, excitement, envy, fear, hate, hope, love, panic, peacefulness, rage, sadness, shame, understanding, and wonder.

- are either primary or secondary. Primary feelings of fear, jealousy, sadness, despair, disappointment, fatigue, and shock frequently get covered up by secondary feelings, such as anger, hopelessness, complacency, laziness, and defensiveness.

- are like electrical charges. They need to be expressed without hurting another person.

- not intellect, blur your objectivity. You are a genius at being objective with other people's children.

- and your level of self-esteem are directly related.

- come from what you believe about yourself, such as how much you respect, regard, value, accept, love, reject, disregard, disrespect, or hate yourself. Your personal and private relationship with yourself greatly affects other relationships. When you love yourself, you feel more peaceful. When you reject yourself, you feel more agitated, critical, impatient, judgmental, and rejecting.

- that you have about yourself might be very different from who you are as a wonderful, valuable, lovable, and worthwhile person.

- that you have about yourself affect how you feel about your children. This was true about your parents when you were a child.

- and behavior are tricky; how you feel inside may be different from how you behave.

- responses and the accompanying familiarity is a way in which history is repeated.

- that you felt as a child may be the same ones you still feel as an adult.

- can be accepted without condoning the behavior which is an expression of the feelings.

- can be transient and not permanent.

- that are kept inside build and increase in intensity; feelings that are expressed lose their intensity.

- sometimes need to be verbalized without engaging in the content. This is true for you and your children.

- are created and controlled by your thinking, and at times that thinking is subconscious. When your thinking becomes conscious, you have control over your feelings and the chances of projecting them onto your kids are decreased.

- Feelings are changed by changing your thinking.

## Your Feelings Are an Important Part of You

Here you are, a wonderful human being, wrapped in a package called "me" which includes your physical body, energy, intelligence, temperament, personality, character traits, beliefs, attitudes, identity, and feelings. You are complex yet simple, separate yet connected, unique yet ordinary. In summary, you are a paradox. Sometimes you know who you are, what you want, what is best for you, and how you feel. Other times you are unsure about who you are, what you want, what is best for you, and how you feel. This is the diversity of your human experience. You spend your lifetime figuring out the answers.

Your children come to you and experience the same diverseness. Is it not amazing that you and your children feel and share any moments of peacefulness and tranquility? Can you imagine what life would be like without feelings?

Your feelings, all of them, are important, and you feel an array of them. Some of them, you experience first (primary) in a situation; others follow and cover them up (secondary).

## You Feel Many Feelings—
## Either Primary or Secondary

The array of feelings you feel is from A to Z. Angry, altruistic, anticipatory, anxious, apathetic, bewildered, confident, courageous, curious, deceived, depressed, disappointed, ecstatic, envious, fearful, generous, hateful, indecisive, jovial, kind, loving, merry, morose, nervous, open, oppressed, optimistic, peaceful, playful, pleasant, quiet, reflective, respectful, repressed, resistant, sad, safe, sorry, tenuous, understood, unloved, violent, vengeful, versatile, willing, wonderful, wild, youthful, and zealous. Feelings are either primary or secondary. You feel the primary one first, and the secondary one next; the secondary emotion covers up the primary emotion. The following are some common examples:

- Your three-year-old carelessly hits you in the eye with a toy; it hurts and you feel pain. You get angry at her. Hurt changes to anger.

- You count on your son to take his usual two-hour nap so you can complete an important task; he sleeps for fifteen minutes and is full of energy. You feel disappointed; you get resentful and irritable. Disappointment changes to resentment.

- You come to school to pick up your daughter; she is not at her usual place and you are frightened. When you find her, you scold her in anger. Fear changes to anger.

- Your son is disappointed that he did not get an invitation to a classmates's birthday party; he converts his disappointment to revenge.

- Your daughter continues to relate to a group of kids who make disrespectful choices and get in trouble frequently. You feel deeply saddened and scared. You say, "I could care less; it is her life." Your sadness and fear change to complacency.

Situations like these include intense feelings, and when you do not stay with your first feeling, as painful as it is, tensions are heightened. When you allow yourself to stay with your primary emotions, you are more open and honest with yourself and your child. When you cover-up your primary emotion, your child never hears your first feeling, and it takes more time to get to the real issues. Time is spent responding to the secondary feeling, and then after some time, getting to the primary one. Do you recall thinking and saying, "Well, I guess I was very hurt, or jealous, or disappointed, or exhausted. I know I sounded angry instead." How often have you made this observation about your child?

The following responses, from the before-mentioned situations, are examples of staying with your primary feeling.

- "My eye hurts. It hurts. It hurts. I feel pain. I need to take care of my eye. I do not want you to swing your toys at anyone. I know that you do not want to hurt me."

- "I am so disappointed that my son did not sleep his usual two-hour nap. I was counting on that time to complete my work. Since children's behavior, at times, is erratic, I need to be very creative in planning when I can get my work done. I am disappointed. Any other day would not have been so crucial. This must be one of the times when being a parent is very inconvenient."

- You find your daughter at a different place and time then usual. You say to her, "Thank goodness, you are safe. I was so scared when I did not see you at our usual meeting place. I was so scared. I love you and want you to be safe. That is the reason I pick you up each day at school."

- Your son tells you that only two boys in his class got an invitation to Philip's birthday party. He tells you how he is planning to get revenge. You say to him, "I know that you are disappointed that Philip did not invite you to his party. Tell me all about your disappointment." (Listen for as long as he needs to express his feelings.) When his feelings are not so intense, tell Philip that you understand and share his disappointment. Ask him if he has any ideas why he was not included? "I am sure there is an understandable explanation. I know that you are feeling disappointed."

- "I feel very frightened and sad about the judgment, choices, and consequences that I see your friends making. It scares me when I hear about them getting into big trouble. I remember, when I was your age, how strong the pressure was to do what friends are doing. I am sad and scared. I want you to use good judgment and not get into trouble. That is what you deserve. I know these are difficult times for you."

As you are more aware of and understand your primary and secondary feelings, you teach the same by your behavior to your children. The power of modeling!

Your focus on your child's primary emotion and not the secondary emotion when it is clear to you, gives a message of understanding to your child about how he is feeling. Understanding denotes acceptance for the first feeling. Focus on the secondary emotion means that you are bypassing your child's first feeling and getting off track. It may feel more intense or painful for both of you to stick with the first feeling; when you do, you make a deeper connection with your child.

A possible stumbling block to listening to and sticking with the primary emotion is the nature of feelings; they have a tendency to obscure your objectivity.

## Your Feelings Blur Your Objectivity

Your feelings are like electrical charges that vary in intensity, depending on the situation. Your waking to a call in the middle of the night and hearing the news that a favorite relative has died creates instant feelings of shock; you remember the time of the call for many years as though it just happened. Your receiving word that you won a contest that you had forgotten about because "I never win anything" brings reactions of euphoria that you remember for a long time. Your experiencing a car accident, where everything happened so fast, leaves you feeling the trauma for months and years, often with you rerunning the scene over and over in your mind. As you recount and share these times, you also feel the feelings.

Feelings during both traumatic and routine times are so strong that your objectivity gets blurred, and your sense of reason and logic is absent for that instant. You cannot be both objective and subjective at the same time. The intensity of your emotions, at that moment, is all-consuming. When the intensity subsides, your reasoning and logic return. Allow yourself to see this difference as a difference; do not label it with any judgment of good, bad, right, or wrong.

Have you noticed how it is different with other people's children? You are a genius at remaining objective with others outside your family. Your feelings are not involved with them as actively as with your family. This explains how it is so easy for others outside your family to give you free and unsolicited advice.

During your high-intensity-feeling times, it is important and helpful for you to talk with people that you trust outside the family to get an objective viewpoint; decisions made, when feelings are running high, are not always ones that you feel good about later. Your self-esteem at these times is tied into your emotions.

## Your Feelings and Self-Esteem are Directly Related

As stated in chapter four "Self-Esteem," you have a private, personal, and on-going relationship with yourself that affects your relationships with others. Remember, your birthright says that you are wonderful, marvelous, and lovely. Others, even your children, see you as wonderful and important, and if you are not believing that you are marvelous, you will not feel wonderful. Your beliefs about you create your feelings which then create your behavior.

Your beliefs and feelings are private, unknown to others, while your behavior is seen by others. What is private and what is seen by others might remind you of an iceberg.

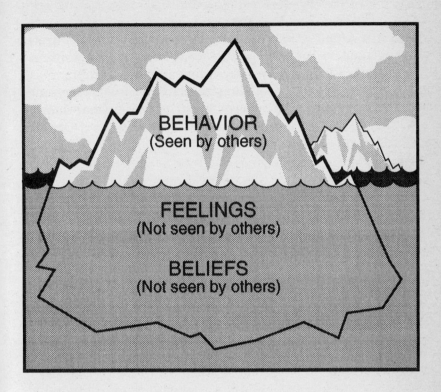

When you believe in yourself and love yourself, you will be at peace. When you reject yourself you become critical, self-effacing, and impatient—you are more harsh with yourself.

Keep in mind that all behavior is interpersonal; how you feel about yourself greatly affects your way of relating to your children. You may attempt to cover up your true feelings, however your children, no matter what their age, can sense your true feelings. Just as you were aware of how your parents were feeling when they thought they were wearing a thick mask. Kids cannot be fooled.

## How You Feel Inside
## May be Different from How You Behave

Young children let you know very clearly how they are feeling. There is no pretense. If she feels upset, she lets you know—even to the point of having a temper tantrum. If he is scared, he with-draws. If she is happy, it shows. The feeling inside is the behavior that you see. This raises an interesting question. How is it that as you grow older your feelings may be different from your behaviors? The answer is in the messages that children receive.

Somewhere in childhood, during the socialization process, children receive messages from adults about feelings. Statements such as, "Don't come out until you can put a smile on your face; You don't have anything to feel down/bad about; Forget about your feelings; They're (your feelings and you) not important; Don't cry over spilled milk: just clean it up; or If you think you have it bad, I'll give you something to feel bad about" reinforce this communication.

Children have not yet learned the ground rule, *Each time I speak, I am saying more about myself than I am saying about you, even though I attach your name to it* to know that parents are talking about what is going on inside them. That is, the parents' behaviors are more a statement about the parents' beliefs and feelings, which they learned growing up, than the child's actions.

Since adults are all-important and children are dependent, children modify their behaviors, doubting their feelings and putting on a facade, to please adults. Their alternative is being themselves, risking judgment, ridicule, or rejection from adults; all this is too scary and emotionally costly for young children. As a result, children hide their feelings and cover them with behaviors they hope are acceptable to their parents. Children grow to adulthood, become parents, share, and teach the same ideas. The cycle continues. When children feel safe, knowing that the adult is accepting and understanding of them and their feelings, their true feelings show.

You might make a distinction among the times, places, and people where it is safe for you to be real and honest with your feelings. Individuals who feel safe behave in ways that are accepting, nonjudgmental, respectful, open, supportive, loving, generous, considerate, and kind. These individual traits provide an atmosphere of safety for you to feel and express your true feelings.

Children are keenly aware of these differences. A five-year-old said it well. "No matter what, Aunt Maddie likes me just the way I am."

Each of you carry your mask with you at all times and put it on at a moment's notice. It is a survival mechanism that you learned as a child. It protects you from feeling too exposed and vulnerable with people who are not accepting and respectful. The feelings from childhood continue to feel familiar and predictable and carry into your adulthood. You respond from these well-known vantage points to your children. Your children copy your behavior and learn from you how to handle their feelings. This history continues.

## History is Repeated Through the Familiarity of Feeling Responses

Do you know how and for what reason you feel certain feelings at specific times? At times your answer is obvious; other times you do not have a clue. How much time do you spend reflecting on how you feel? Given how your feelings detract from your objectivity, it is an easier task to speculate how and for what reason your children are feeling certain ways. Yet, given the interpersonal nature and significance of your relationship with your children, the main answers are within you; answers that come from understanding what feelings were familiar for you as a child.

→ **As a Child Did You Feel:**

- upset when you wanted to sleep in your parent's bed and your father took you to your bed?

- excited and grown-up when you stayed at grandma and grandpa's house without your older brother?

- protected when your parents would not allow your little sister to come into your room without your permission?

- angry when your sister got more of your mother's attention and you felt that your mother loved your sister more than you?

- left out when you wanted to play hide-and-seek with the big kids and they ran away and left you?

- jealous when your twin brother learned to ride a two-wheeler before you did?

- violated when your uncle crossed personal boundaries, took advantage of your innocence and sexually abused you?

- accepted when your father listened to your view of the situation?

- cheated when you were restricted from active play and sports because you had asthma?

- sad when your grandmother died and left out when your mother thought you were too young to attend the funeral?

- powerless and uprooted when your family moved each year, and you spent much of your time saying hello and goodbye?

- relieved when your parents fought and told you their fighting was not about or because of you?

- excited, beyond sleep, the night before your family vacation to Disney World?

- betrayed when your best friend selected another best friend?

- depressed because you admired and emulated your mother's love and skill of reading, knowing how hard your reading disability made it for you to read like her?

- hurt and let down when your parents broke a promise that was important to you?

- resigned and overpowered when your mother always insisted that you "Do it her way?"

- abandoned when your father left and did not talk to you because your parents were having problems?

- panicked when your mother went to the hospital in the middle of the night for emergency surgery?

- unappreciated and demoralized when you followed the rules and still got criticized?

- sad when your pet rabbit died, and you were told to keep busy and forget about it?

- ridiculed for the way you spoke before your corrective mouth surgery?

- happy to have the same best friend through twelve years of public school?

- surprised when you got a scholarship to go to a prestigious college?

Which of these feelings did you experience most?

Which happened infrequently?

What do you think was the long-term effect of these events?

What meaning (beliefs about you) do you give to these feelings or what do you think they say about you?

What are the major themes?

Are they adequacy, inadequacy, worthiness, worthlessness, responsibility, irresponsibility, pride, shame, anxiety, peacefulness, depression, fear, contentment, powerlessness, powerfulness, or boldness?

Which do you still carry with you?

What effect do these emotions have on your current functioning, including how you respond to your children?

When you were a child, were there times and situations where adults or peers took advantage of your vulnerability or dependency, and you felt violated, cheated, unappreciated, powerless, betrayed, diminished, demoralized, shamed or ridiculed? Did your parents (or another adult) tell you that it was not you, rather it was more about what was going on inside the other person? At times when your parents (as happens with all parents) were upset about their own matters, did they tell you clearly that it was not you? Now do you keep these clear and respectful boundaries with your children?

The predominant feelings that were familiar for you as a child may still be with you as an adult. I hear parents say, "I know I am an adult, yet in many ways I still feel like a child." You may even use the same manner to express your feelings that you used as a child. Do you know that you can accept your children and their feelings without liking or condoning the behavior which is an expression of those feelings? Do you know that difference about yourself?

## You Can Accept Feelings
## Without Condoning the Behavior
## That is an Expression of the Feelings

Of the many clarifications that I make with parents, none is more frequent than the confusion between feelings and the manner in which those feelings are expressed. This confusion conveys false messages to children:

- your feelings are not good or right,

- you should not feel what you are feeling,

- since your behavior, an expression of your feelings, is not okay, then you are not okay,

- keep your feelings inside; I cannot handle them (or you),

- you are too emotional.

Your child's behavior is obvious to you and others; understanding the feelings that create the behavior is less obvious. You spend much time concerned about your child's behavior. You are a genius at describing, critiquing, criticizing, judging, worrying about, and reacting to your child's behavior. The more difficult and challenging task is understanding the feelings and beliefs that support the behavior. As children sense that their feelings are understood, it is easier for them to change their behavior. The following example of Adam shows how his parents struggled to separate accepting his feelings without condoning his behavior, a manifestation of his feelings.

### Adam

Ten-year-old Adam had the energy of two kids. As a young child, he stopped taking daytime naps when he was two and was always on-the-go. Occasionally he played with sedentary toys like Legos or Tinker toys, yet most of the time he preferred large motor activities like running and jumping. He was always moving. Conversely, at bedtime, he was sound asleep as soon as his head hit the pillow and he slept well.

However, Adam was apprehensive about new situations. He felt anxiety that was as intense as the energy he expended in his favorite activities. His usual energy levels were heightened when he was in a new situation. His mother said that during these times he would talk incessantly, cling to adults, and in general be out-of-control. Once he felt comfortable in the situation, his behavior returned to his usual energy levels.

Obviously, his parents were embarrassed by Adam's annoying actions in new situations and did not want to accept his behavior. They had some insight into his feelings, so it was easier for them to accept and understand how his anxiety and energy levels were increased in situations where he felt some discomfort.

To let Adam know that they accepted his feelings and not his behavior, they said to him, "Adam, we know that you are a wonderful son and you have lots of energy. You amaze us at times with how active you are. We would love to have some of your energy. We have noticed that when you are in situations where you don't know people or are feeling unsure about what might happen or what is expected of you that your energy levels go sky-high. At those times you talk and talk, hang on to adults, and get out-of-control. That must feel awful for you when you feel so much nervousness and anxiety. We want you to know that we understand those feelings. The next time before you are in a new situation, perhaps we can talk about it before you go and after you get home. That might help with your strong feelings."

As Adam's parents understood and accepted his feelings, Adam's feelings of anxiety in new situations shifted to feelings of excitement of self-control.

When you do not like or understand your child's behavior, you need to probe beyond the actions to get a sense of how your child might be feeling. At times, this is obvious and at times more difficult. Behavior is best understood in the context of the child's age, developmental stage, temperament, likes and dislikes, and historical and recent experiences. Your eight or eleven-year-old will have different reactions and feelings from your seventeen-year-old.

Probing more deeply and keeping in mind the bigger context allows you to help your child reach her feelings and express them. Feelings need to be felt and expressed in ways that do not hurt or violate others. You know how good you feel when you talk with someone who listens and understands you; you can "get it off of your chest" and know that you are still loved.

## Feelings That Are Kept Inside
## Build and Increase in Intensity—
## Feelings That Are Expressed Lose Their Intensity

Feelings need to be expressed to decrease their intensity. Conversely, storing them inside allows them to build and build; they come out at times and in ways that are disproportionate to what is happening at the moment. You know what happens if you hold the lid tightly on a boiling tea kettle. When feelings are kept inside, the stored intensity comes out in ways that may be hurtful to others. A ten-year-old told me, "When I don't get it out with the people I'm mad at, I take it out on innocent people who don't deserve it. Then I feel worse."

Every incident in your life that has happened to you, and everything that you have observed or done has accompanying thoughts, perceptions, reactions, and feelings. For every event, you feel a feeling. It is from these countless experiences that you have learned what is painful, soothing, joyful, scary, sad, pleasant, exciting, important, trivial, dangerous, safe, and enraging. From these feeling responses, you attached a certain meaning to people, events, and situations that stays with you and generalizes to other events in your life.

For example, suppose when you were four-years-old you were suddenly surprised and bitten by a dog that seemed to come out of nowhere. As a result of this experience, your perception of dogs undoubtedly would be different than had you not been bitten. Yet, you do not feel fear, surprise, and pain all the time—only when you encounter a dog. Maybe your reaction is even more specific in that you feel surprise, fear, and pain only when you see the specific type of dog that bit you, and your reaction is not generalized to all dogs. You may have suppressed the memory of the event, yet your feelings do not let you forget what you felt.

Maybe you grew up with constant criticism about what you did and did not do. You did not know that it was not you; it was what was going on inside your parents because they grew up with constant criticism. You felt diminished (criticism is diminishing) and angry.

What might have changed the above dog-scene is the active presence of one adult who was there when the dog bit you. The adult's active presence includes: understanding that certain experiences evoke specific and strong feelings, validating your feelings (what you feel is OK), listening without criticism, judgment, and impatience as you express your feelings, knowing the value of voicing feelings without getting caught in the content, and not sermonizing about the situation. Sermonizing means giving reasons, justifications, explanations, admonitions; none of these are helpful when feelings need to be expressed. In addition, the adult's role is to let the child know in a clear statement if the happening was or was not because of the child. In this example, the child had nothing to do with getting bitten except for being there.

In the above scene, an active, present adult would say, "I know how surprising, scary, and painful it is for a dog to come from behind you and bite you. You did not see him coming. It is not because of you that he bit you. It was the dog. You did not cause the dog to bite you. That nasty dog. It is not you. You can feel all of your feelings for as long as you need to. You have to feel the feelings and get them out. They are OK. It is surprising, scary, and painful to get bitten by a dog. When those surprising, scary, and painful feelings come again, please come and tell me about them. I want to hear your feelings and I understand."

If the event happened because of the child, wait until the feelings are expressed and some healing has taken place before you talk about what lessons can be learned so there is not a repeat event. Suppose the child in the above scene had pulled the dog's tail and then was bitten. After the initial feelings are expressed, you say, "I know that this a hard lesson for you to learn and it is a painful lesson. The lesson is important. When you pull a dog's tail, there is a chance the dog will not like it and will bite you. I know this is a tough lesson."

When you experience another's feelings that has nothing to do with you and is not directed at you, some of your own feelings may be stimulated. You are human. An example is your teenage son storming into the house feeling upset about his car breaking down again. He is not hurting you or other family members, yet his ventilation is affecting you. What can you do?

First, know that he needs to express and release his feelings. Stored feelings come out in such ways as projection, displacement, blaming, and loudness. Second, keep remembering that the situation has nothing to do with you. It is his issue and responsibility. If you get involved, you compound the intensity of the moment and cross over your boundary. Third, know that some feelings are transient and not permanent. Fourth, if you need to voice your feelings, find a place and time (your back woods, car, or attic) where your expression will not affect anyone. It is a popular myth that others always need to be present in order for you to air your feelings. Sometimes you need to get it out with no one there. It is more for your benefit than anyone else.

Feelings can stay with you for a long time depending on whether someone helped you to accept and express them at the time of the event. It is possible, years later, to accept and express feelings that have been stored. This is the benefit of counseling and psychotherapy. All that you have experienced (lived, felt, observed, participated in) is part of you now. If you decide that you want to change any of your feelings, that is in your control by changing your thinking.

## You Change Your Feelings by Changing Your Thinking

You are the only one in charge of your thinking. Your feelings are in your control and can be changed as you change your thinking. *I am responsible for and to myself and I create my own experiences and feelings*. If you believe that others control your thoughts, you give your power away. It may seem like you do not have control over your thoughts since some of your thinking occurs at an unconscious level. Many of your experiences, both painful and happy, are stored in your subconsciousness. What is conscious for you feels more like it is in your control than what is not conscious.

To change a feeling, it is necessary to identify the accompanying belief and change it. The following are some common examples.

The feeling to change is listed first and is followed by the thought change.

- From powerless to empowered—Change thoughts of I am no one to thoughts of I am worthwhile and important.

- From inadequacy to adequacy—Change thoughts of I never do anything right to I can learn to do many things right,

- From anxiety to peacefulness—Change thoughts of I am a bundle of nerves to I am and deserve peacefulness.

- From punishment to freedom—Change thoughts of I deserve punishment to I do not deserve to be punished.

- From fear to love—Change thoughts of I am tense and scared to I accept the wonderful person who I am.

Say the new thought over and over in a sincere way. It will feel awkward and untrue at first, yet keep repeating it to yourself. Your thoughts dictate your feelings, and eventually you will start feeling the new way. Whenever you think in the old ways, identify it as just that and change your thought. Be gentle with yourself, understanding that habits are challenging, yet possible to break. And remember, *At any time, I am doing the best that I can do.* After awhile, you will notice your beliefs changing also, and it will not seem like such hard work. Know that you are well deserving of all the respect and peacefulness you create.

### → For Your Journal

Label a section in your journal "Feelings." Start by listing all of the different ways that you feel or have felt in your life. Is there a feeling you experience most of the time, or with certain people, or in certain settings? How do you describe yourself regarding your feelings? Become more sensitive to the spectrum of feelings in you.

As you become more aware of your feelings, watch for your primary feelings and your secondary feelings. Challenge yourself to stick more with the feeling you have first and note the differences. This will make you more sensitive to your children's feelings and help you to teach them to stay with their first ones.

Note how your feelings change when your self-esteem is low due to stress, fatigue, or overload. What changes do you see? Note how that is also true for your children.

Identify with whom you can share your inner feelings and know that you will be loved and accepted. How do you mask your feelings when it is not safe to be honest with how you are really feeling inside?

Note how you felt much of the time as a child? Has that feeling changed much for you as an adult? What impact does that feeling have on you now and your children?

Identify what feelings you are willing to let go of and change. Write what belief supports your feeling. Create a new belief, repeating it over and over. Keep track of the changes you feel. If you have difficulty, identify what is getting in the way.

→ **Remember . . .**

- Your feelings are a wonderful part of you.

- It is impossible for you to understand and accept you and your child's feelings too much.

- Accepting your feelings, without guilt or judgment, allows you to create changes.

- Your feelings are not poured in concrete and can change frequently.

- Feelings that are stored take their toll in many ways that are more costly and painful than expressing them initially.

- Your feelings are powerful and are in your control.

- Only you can change your feelings—even if it is your reaction to something that someone else does.

**Chapter 10 Overview**

**Five Parenting Tools: Praise, Affirmation, Encouragement, Criticism, and Judgement**

- Praise, Affirmation, Encouragement, Criticism, and Judgement are Parenting Tools
- Praise, Affirmation, and Encouragement Are the Opposite of Criticism and Judgment
- Defining and Using Praise
- Defining and Using Affirmation
- Defining and Using Encouragement
- Defining and Using Criticism and Judgment
- For Your Journal
- Remember . . .

# 10

# Five Parenting Tools: Praise, Affirmation, Encouragement, Criticism, and Judgment

## Points to Ponder

- Praise, affirmation, encouragement, criticism, and judgment are parenting tools; each has its own effect.

- Praise, affirmation, and encouragement are the opposite of criticism and judgment.

- Praise, affirmation, and encouragement are your tools for teaching respect, peacefulness, patience, tolerance, acceptance, and cooperation. Criticism and judgment teach defiance, disapproval, faultfinding, antagonism, and belligerence.

- Praise, affirmation, and encouragement bring out the best in you and your children. Criticism and judgment bring out the worst.

- Praise, affirmation, and encouragement have slight and consequential differences in their definition, usage, and outcomes. It is important that you know the differences. You can never have too many finely-tuned tools in your parenting tool kit.

- Praise focuses on the person, behaviors, performance, and achievement. Affirmation focuses on the person, and encouragement gives messages of support, assurance, confidence, hopefulness, and inspiration.

- Praise, affirmation, and encouragement are experienced by children as genuine when given in moderation. Excessiveness and superlatives feel insincere to children.

- Praise is an antidote to discouragement, criticism, blame, ridicule, and condemnation; affirmation is an antidote to disapproval and judgment; encouragement is an antidote to discouragement and hopelessness.

### Praise, Affirmation, Encouragement, Criticism, and Judgment are Parenting Tools

You have many ways to parent and many tools to use. Your tools are the different ways of relating to your children; each has its own focus and outcome. The five most common ones are praise, affirmation, encouragement, criticism, and judgment. You bring the tools with you that were applied to you as a child and continue to use them with your children because they are familiar. As stated before, familiarity is powerful.

Most likely, you are aware of the effects of each tool for yourself and your child. Some you like and some you do not like, yet liking or disliking is not as influential as familiarity. You are a creature of habit even when your best judgment, common sense, and logical thinking are saying something different to you. In other words, you might find yourself being critical with yourself and your child, knowing the effects of criticism, yet continuing the same behaviors.

I remember a young mother who was overwhelmed with feelings as she shared how she identified her daughter's biting response of "I can't do anything right for you" as one that she remembers thinking frequently and saying occasionally to her mother. She recalled that her response followed her mother saying, "Will you ever get it right?" As this young mother listened to herself, she sounded just like her mother.

People who visit a mental health professional have often experienced more criticism and judgment than praise, affirmation, and encouragement. Many realize that they were recipients of criticism and judgment as children who, in their most honest moments, know the pain, yet they continue to be critical and judgmental of their children. It takes awareness, hard work, practice, self-forgiveness, (for falling into the old patterns) and self-discipline to change these familiar, historical patterns and habits.

Frequently, you as parents share with me that, in the middle of an interaction with your child, an awareness flashes about which tool you are using. The flash might be a prompt to use another tool or to continue with what is familiar. If only the same ease were available to you as when a carpenter decides to switch from one tool to another tool when the one that was selected first is not working well or is not producing the desired results. Think of this analogy as you learn more about the fine differences and effects between the tools that you use to relate to your children. Changing tools is in your control.

## Praise, Affirmation, and Encouragement are the Opposite of Criticism and Judgment

The differences between praise, affirmation, and encouragement are knowing whether to use a pipe wrench or pliers to open a rusted faucet; whereas, the difference between praise, affirmation, encouragement versus criticism and judgement is knowing that a steel tape measure will not do what a hammer will do. Knowing the differences between what the particular tools do is equally as important as knowing what you want.

Most of you have a general idea of what you want for your children. I hear no confusion about this. I do hear confusion, in practice, about how to get what you want. Keep in mind that what you want might be quite different from what you experienced as a child.

As you understand these important tools, what each is and does, you can decide which one you want to use at any given time. How you relate to your children can never be too finely tuned.

## Defining and Using Praise

Praise is a way of communicating approval, admiration, valuing, applause, compliments, congratulations, or honor to your child, his/her behavior, or accomplishment. Praise says:

- You are wonderful.

- I love your big hug.

- I know you can ride your tricycle all by yourself.

- I see that you can write your name.

- Thank you for keeping your hands to yourself.

- I know that you got all of your homework assignment completed and correct.

- The flowers you picked and arranged in the vase look nice.

- The napkin holder you designed and made is very attractive.

- The essay you wrote shows mature, critical thinking.

Praise is a way of paying attention to your children in a way that meets their recognition needs while it provides support for themselves, their behavior, accomplishments, and achievements.

Praise is a common, parenting tool that is used in specific and general ways, moderate and excessive ways, and genuine and insincere ways. A specific usage is saying to your three-year-old, "I like the way you put on your shoes and socks on all by yourself." A general usage is saying to your fifteen-year-old, "I appreciate the responsible manner in which you are taking charge of your school work and your home duties."

Moderate usage involves selecting the situations where you choose to use praise thus allowing your children the opportunity to learn to praise themselves at other times.

Excessive means using praise much of the time for everything. Children tell me that when their parent's praise is in moderation, it sounds more genuine than when it is excessive with too many superlatives. When you use praise excessively, your children become dependent on you and avoid learning how to praise themselves. Too much of anything, no matter how valuable it maybe can create dependency. Dependency is the opposite of what your children need to develop and maintain as they grow.

Parents often err on the side of too little praise or excessive praise. Your challenge is to find a moderate balance.

A guide to help you with moderation is to ask yourself how important the situation, action, performance, or achievement is to your child as opposed to how important it is to you. If it is important to your child, use praise. For children under five, assume that any situation with a significant adult or any opportunity to increase independence is important. Children five years and older have developed some definite likes and preferences.

For example, if you know that learning to ride a bicycle without training wheels is very important to your five-year- old, praise his successes. When your ten-year-old daughter, who wants to control her temper, tells you that she needs to go to her room and cool down, praise her. Look for the small steps that your child makes toward self-control and mastery. Children need genuine praise every day, and as for adults, what matters the most has the most meaning.

In addition to the importance to your child is asking the following questions: Is this situation or event a time for my child to develop more esteem, self-control, mastery, creativity, independence, or recognition? Are there safety lessons that my child needs to learn? Are there coping skills that can be learned so she can function more peacefully in her interpersonal relationships? Answering these questions helps you to praise in moderate and meaningful ways.

Not every tool is useful for every situation that you experience with your children. There are those times when praise is inadequate; the tool beyond praise is affirmation.

## Defining and Using Affirmation

The tool of affirmation is helpful at those times when you honestly cannot praise either your child's actions or performance. You have experienced the quandary of knowing that you are dishonest with yourself if you give praise when you know that your child's behavior or performance is not worthy of praise. However, you know that your child is in need of being recognized, valued, or appreciated; your child is feeling awful inside and his behaviors are out-of-control, rude, non-productive, or disruptive. For you, as for your children, there are those times when it feels like everything goes wrong and nothing turns out the way you want it to.

Affirmation is a wonderful tool to use when you want to say *"yes"* to your child, knowing that you cannot honestly say *"yes"* to his actions or achievements. Affirmation is a way of saying that I accept you as a person even though I chose not to accept, value, support, or approve of your behavior or actions at this moment. This is the time that your child needs to hear that she is valued and loved just because she exists. This is a very critical distinction for you to understand.

Parents get confused about this distinction and fear that they are reinforcing disrespectful behaviors. You can accept your child without accepting the behavior that is a manifestation of how your child is feeling at that moment. In other words, when you meet your child's need to be affirmed, you are not reinforcing the behavior that is coming from his unmet need for affirmation. Your child is always a wonderful person despite her actions. Affirmation focuses on the wonderful person he is, even though he is not feeling or acting in wonderful ways.

You understand the difference between the person and behavior to the degree to which you accept yourself when you behave in ways that are the opposite of who you are as a wonderful person. Your ability to accept and tolerate yourself when you do not like your behavior affects your ability to be affirming of your children when their behavior is not respectful or pleasing. Ironically, that is the time when you and your children need the most acceptance and affirmation.

Affirmation is needed most when your child is feeling discouraged, and her behavior is out-of-control or disrespectful. If you think about the times when you are experiencing these feelings, you know the value and impact of a friend reaching out to you with kindness, love, appreciation and generosity. Ironically, for you and your child, these are the times when your behaviors are not inviting what you need.

Affirmation involves sensing how your child is feeling and then looking beyond the behaviors and actions to find something to affirm. It is so easy to see just the actions and react in kind to them. Rudeness invites rudeness and disrespect invites disrespect. Remember, the behavior that you see is only a manifestation of how your child is feeling at a given time.

The following are examples of what you can affirm:

- effort, energy, drive, working hard
- willingness to take a risk, try, attempt
- generosity
- kindness, thoughtfulness, graciousness
- perseverance, tenacity, endurance, (sticking with tasks)
- listening
- offering to help
- support
- presence and being there
- giving consideration for his/her ideas
- giving time
- patience
- keeping eye contact
- holding still
- caring
- pleasantness
- gentleness
- sensitivity and empathy
- talking (as opposed to remaining silent)

The following situations present opportunities to use affirmation.

- Your two-year-old keeps taking the washcloths that you folded neatly and stacked and throws them on the floor. Before you can pick them up, he has moved to the stack of socks that you just sorted and paired, pulls them apart and throws them on the floor. He then goes back to the wash cloths that you restacked, grabs several and throws them in the playpen with his eight-month-old sister. You do not want to reinforce any of his out-of-control behavior, even though he is only two, so you say, "What limitless energy you have. I know it will take you far in life." You then get him interested in playing with some blocks and quickly put away the clothes.

- Your five-year-old has been a finicky eater, and you are concerned about her nutrition since there are so few fruits and vegetables she will eat. You know not to get into a power struggle over food. You prepare an attractive tray with different fresh vegetables that are cut in interesting shapes. You pass the tray to your daughter who selects a carrot curl. She takes two bites and puts the rest on her plate. You would like to lecture her about how she needs to eat more vegetables, instead you use affirmation and say, "I appreciate the way you took several bites from the carrot. Isn't that neat the way it was curled?" You think to yourself: I see that, on her own, she took a risk and ate a few bites of carrot.

- Your eight-year-old knows that you lost your job when your company moved from your town. He overheard you talking with his father about your financial concerns about paying the bills. He gives you one dollar and thirty-four cents from his piggy bank to help. You do not want to take his money, so you say, "Thank you for being so generous with your money. You are very kind and thoughtful. I know you want to help. Your father and I will figure out how to take care of our finances. That is our job. I want you to keep on saving your money. I know you worked hard for it."

- Your ten-year-old daughter cannot wait until she is fifteen years old like her sister. Every time her sister has a friend over, your ten-year-old insists on being in the same room with them. If she is playing outside with her ten-year-old friends and her older sister comes home, she leaves her friends to follow her sister. Of course, no fifteen-year-old wants to be shadowed by her ten-year-old sister. You cannot support what she is doing and the conflict it causes, yet you can say, "I noticed that you have much perseverance. Even though your sister does not want you with her and her friends, you do not give up. Perseverance is a wonderful trait. You do not deserve the constant rejection you get from your sister. I want you to ask your sister if she wants you to be with her and, if not, to find some of your friends to play with. I know that it is hard being the younger sister."

- Your thirteen-year-old son is adamant about buying a pair a boots that you feel are too expensive and impractical. You sense that he is responding to peer pressure and will find the boots uncomfortable, and they will sit in his closet. You let him know how you understand how much he wants them now because his two best friends have a pair and he likes the style. As you listen, you sense he is becoming more calm and is listening to your reservations about the boots. You say to him, "Thank you for listening to me. I know that we have different ways of seeing the boots."

- Your seventeen-year-old, into her final physical and psychological separation, frequently opposes what you say. Most of the issues are small ones, such as preference for salad dressing, the best place to buy car gas, who makes the best pizza, how to clean the kitchen, and which toothpaste is best. Even though her oppositional behavior reminds you of the time when she was two-years-old, you understand that it is not a bid for a power struggle, rather it is a statement of her autonomy and independence. Your response to her is, "I know when you are on your own that you have the self-sufficiency skills to do well. You know what you want and take charge."

Use your creativity to look beneath your child's behavior for what you can affirm. In any situation, it is possible to find something to affirm. Receiving affirmation helps to meet needs of recognition, acceptance, and approval.

Encouragement, a closely-related tool, goes beyond praise and affirmation and is helpful when your child is learning and maintaining new skills.

# Defining and Using Encouragement

Encouragement is synonymous with being a cheerleader. Your child is on the playing field, playing the game, and you are on the sidelines saying that I know you can do it, Keep hanging in there, I am on your side, Go for it, You'll make it, and I believe in you. Encouragement inspires, motivates, stimulates, promotes, and is an antidote to discouragement.

Perhaps you remember people from your childhood who were encouraging to you, and you value the people in your adult life who encourage you, especially at times when you need a boost. Those individuals are vivid in your memory and are very special to you. Encouragement is a precious gift.

Encouragement is most useful when your child is learning a new skill. Once you learn and become proficient at a task, you quickly forget the process, sometimes painstaking, that you went through to learn how to master the task. Children benefit from support as each step is mastered.

Think about some of your first experiences, such as, holding a crayon, cutting paper, tying your shoes, talking on the telephone, riding a bike, wrapping a present, using a camera, addressing an envelope, baking cookies, learning to use computers, giving a speech, framing a picture, ironing a garment, peeling potatoes, raking leaves, using a pocket knife, and driving a car. Remember how conscious each step and move was for you and how much you practiced. Now many years later, you do not have to stop and think about each and every move you make. It is so familiar; it is part of you.

Encouragement entails trusting that your child can learn the steps involved to master a task or skill. Then you are cheering, applauding, reassuring, and supporting until his/her goal is reached.

Praise, affirmation, and encouragement are different ways of giving your child feedback about her person, behavior, and accomplishments. As constructive and helpful as praise, encouragement, and affirmation are, one caution about dependency needs to be noted. Children can become too dependent on these tools as external validation sources of themselves, therefore, not developing their own internal validation skills. The goal as you use these tools is to support and validate your child by giving him feedback about himself, his actions, and his performance to aid him in learning to praise, affirm, and encourage himself as he grows to adulthood.

Growing up for your child means slowly acquiring tools for her tool kit. Some tools build, support, and enhance your child's development of herself and some tools destroy. The tools of praise, affirmation, and encouragement are the antithesis of criticism and judgment.

## Defining and Using Criticism and Judgment

Each of you has experienced being criticized or judged. No one who lives on our planet escapes it. You know how it feels and what it does to you. As a child, your options were limited about how much to allow other's criticism and judgment to affect you. As an adult, your challenge is to remember that the person criticizing or judging is really telling you more about what is going on inside of him/her than he/she is saying anything about you.

Criticism and judgment hurt and humiliate your children. Parents who criticize and judge teach their children to criticize and judge. No parent intends or wants this to happen to their children: the likely explanation is that history is speaking loudly. Parents who received judgment and criticism as children use the same tools with their children.

Parents who believe that they are very important people and are in charge of their experiences and feelings, change rather than repeat their histories. Never easy, yet possible.

Criticism and judgment are expressed in both direct and indirect ways. Some forms are teasing, sarcasm, comparison, humor or jest, ridicule, insult, taunting, mockery, harassment, and shaming. The critical or judgmental message can be obvious or hidden; the impact is the same however it is delivered.

The phrase "constructive criticism" is common and is confusing for parents. Some parents interpret constructive criticism as a justification for being critical. Yet, criticism is criticism and judgment is judgment. What I hear parents asking for is a way to give their children feedback about their thinking or actions so that their child does not feel criticized or judged. An important role in parenting is reflecting to your children what they are doing and teaching them more respectful actions. Learning that enhances your child's well-being does not happen in a atmosphere of judgment and criticism. The distinction between feedback and criticism is an important one.

The following statements are experienced by children as critical or judgmental. The response in parentheses is what children would like to say if given a chance.

- "You should be ashamed of yourself." (I am still a child and sometimes I forget about all of the rules. Be patient with me while I learn to remember the rules. Your shaming me makes me feel anxious and rejected and certainly does not help me to remember.)

- "Your brother never acted that way when he was your age." (I am me. I am not my brother. Please accept me and do not compare me with anyone else.)

- "I thought you knew better." (Where you are with "knowing better" and where I am with "knowing better" are different. I know adults who "know better" and their behavior doesn't change. I need time to practice and maintain my "knowing better" behaviors.)

- "You just wait until your father comes home." (I hate to be threatened. My father is not here to see the whole picture. Please feel strong enough within yourself to teach me the behaviors that are good for me now. Please speak for yourself, mother, and deal with me directly. Both of us deserve that respect.)

- "How could you do such a dumb thing?" (Probably because I am a kid. I am still learning how to take charge of myself. When I do a "dumb thing" I have a chance to learn more about my actions and accept and forgive myself. Those are three wonderful assets.)

- "You never get anything right." (I know when you are upset and feeling frustrated that you get impatient with me and then your reaction to me is extreme. I hear you use extreme words such as never, always, anything, and everything. I do get some things right. I am still learning many skills and benefit more when you are patient with yourself and me.)

Just as critical or judgmental is a scornful look, silence, and obviously harsh, stinging words. All say more about the person delivering the message than the person who is receiving the message. All hurt and destroy.

In contrast, it is possible and helpful for you to give your children feedback about themselves, their thinking, actions and behaviors, choices and decisions, and activities. The best way to give feedback is to say, "I want to tell you something important that I noticed about you." Proceed to share your feedback in clear and specific terms.

For example, "I noticed that when you wait until close to bedtime to start your homework that you do not do it as thoroughly as when you begin it earlier. You deserve to do your best." Your child will hear that you are giving feedback when you start your conversation with "I noticed that . . ., I observed that . . ., I see when . . ., My observation is (or has been), I feel concerned when I hear you say or see you . . . and I am not sure if you know when you are . . . ."

Children are so busy with their own growth and development and often so consumed by their needs (because they are kids) that they do not know how what they are doing is impacting on themselves and others. This is often true for adults. Feedback that is honest, nonjudgmental, and respectful can teach children to take more responsibility for themselves.

### → For Your Journal

Identify the tool(s), praise, affirmation, encouragement, criticism, or judgment most frequently used on you when you were a child. By whom? When? How do you think that person was feeling? What was going on inside him/her at that time? What was your reaction to each way of relating? Which have been destructive or conducive to your well-being?

Identify which tool(s) you use most with your children. When do you use them? How do you identify which tool to use? Is the determining factor your child's behavior or what is going on inside of you? How do you feel after you use each tool? How do you want your relationship with your child to be different? How can you change your ways of relating and using the tools that will strengthen, not defeat, your child?

Reflect and write about these five tools weekly. Critique your behavior in an open and accepting manner. Know that you are the only one who can change your relationship with your children to be more peaceful and respectful.

## → Remember . . .

- You can never have too many tools in your parenting tool kit or be too familiar with what each does.

- How you or your children behave at any given moment is the expression of feelings inside.

- It is better for you to err on the side of too much praise, affirmation, and encouragement than too much criticism and judgment.

- Criticism and judgment are used by well-meaning parents; it is their unresolved hurt from childhood passed on to their children.

- Your children, like you, are tender and sensitive.

- You can relate in any way to your children that you choose. In other words, you select your tool.

**Chapter II, Overview**

**Conflict in the Parent-Child Relationship**

- What is the Conflict About?
- Conflict is a Predictable Way of Creating Emotional Distance for Self-Protection
- Conflict Does Not Come From Your Child's Behavior
- Conflict is Learned and Comes From Unmet Needs or Unfulfilled Expectations
- How You Think May be Different From How You Feel
- How to Decrease Conflict
- For Your Journal
- Remember . . .

# 11

## Conflict in the Parent-Child Relationship

### Conflict:

- is a learned, not inherited, process.

- is the opposite of peacefulness.

- is the struggle between what you need or want and what someone wants and needs who is significant to you.

- is interpersonal. That is, the degree to which your parents' childhood needs were fulfilled is directly related to their ability to meet your needs.

- is individual and personal. That is, what might be conflictive for you may not be a conflict for another person.

- that you felt as a child was decreased or intensified first by the importance of your need and second by the degree of satisfaction of the need that you felt.

- that you experienced as a child when you felt powerless and dependent necessitated that you learn behaviors to protect yourself.

- that you experienced as a child taught you how safe it is to be close or distant from people in primary relationships, and therefore, you learned how to regulate your behavior to invite closeness or distance. From this experience you created beliefs and attitudes to manage your behaviors.

- arises from unmet needs or unfulfilled expectations.

- does not come from the other person's behavior; it is what happens within you. This idea is most contrary to popular thinking.

- in the parent-child relationship, like beauty, is in the definition, experience, familiarity, control, and eye of the beholder. In other words, conflict between you and your child comes from your perception of and the meaning that you give to what is happening at the moment.

- is decreased as you remember that the other person is talking about his/her experience even though he/she projects his/her feelings onto you. In other words, hear the feelings without personalizing the content.

- does not come from badness. There are no bad people, only people who believe that they are bad.

- decreases as you take a look at and more responsibility for what is happening within you.

- is decreased to the degree that one or both participants take ownership for his/her unmet needs.

- is best understood as you know about integrity, self-esteem, personal boundaries, the process (what is happening between two people), and the content (what is being fought about).

## What is the Conflict About?

When there is a conflict between you and your child, what is the conflict about? Your first response, like many parents' response is, "It was something that my child did. It is she. It is he." This view of conflict overlooks the importance of the experiences that you bring to your parenting from your childhood and the impact of your background on your children. Conflict is learned and perpetuated in the arena of the parent-child relationship. Conflict is first felt within you and then affects the other person. When you are peaceful within yourself, your response to your children is different from the times when you are feeling inner turmoil.

You have experienced conflict from the moment you were born, yet you do not remember consciously the first time you felt the inner turmoil and uncomfortable feelings. Struggling to breathe, adjusting to life outside the womb, signaling that you were hungry before you had the words to speak, shivering to regulate your body temperature, squirming when the blanket was wrapped too tightly, crying when bounced beyond your limits, squinting to protect your eyes from the bright lights, feeling cramps in your stomach, and sensing that the milk you are fed is too hot or too cold were your first experiences of conflict.

The list continues: Wanting to sleep when Aunt Martha and Uncle Rick stop by unexpectedly for a visit and your parents awakened you "to show you off"; Wanting to watch the mobile that sparkled in the sunlight when you are turned on your stomach for a nap; Wanting to wear your comfortable sneakers to the family reunion and being told that you have to wear your patent leather strap shoes "to be dressed up"; Needing time to learn to know your cousins who have returned from overseas and feeling forced to play with them now "because they are your relatives and the adults know each other"; Declaring some wonderful five-year-old independence and being told that you are a "show-off";

Wanting to be best friends with another kid in your class and her not wanting to have anything to do with you; Wanting to cry when your grandfather died and your father saying with his behavior "males don't cry"; Wanting to take calculus because you love math and your brother putting you down because "he is jealous of your ability";

Needing to organize and complete your school work in a way that makes sense to you and being told that you are stubborn and oppositional; Needing understanding and forgiveness when you make mistakes and instead receiving shame and ridicule; Needing to take more control over your life and hearing that all you think about is yourself; Needing privacy when the other person needs closeness; Needing to talk when the other person needs quiet time.

The conflict is a clash and struggle between what you need and want versus what someone wants who is significant to you. The internal struggle is a deep fear that your needs will not be met and that what is important to you for your growth and well-being will be overlooked. Children, being powerless and dependent, count on important adults to meet their needs. Adults, being humans who grew up with parents unable to meet all of their needs, unwittingly, and unintentionally do not always meet all of their children's needs.

Conflict, therefore, is personal and individual. Simply stated, what is conflictive for you may not be conflictive for another person. The degree of inner conflict that the child experiences is related first to the importance of the need to the child and second to the degree of satisfaction that the need is met. Physical needs for food, water, shelter, and elimination require satisfaction before needs of recognition, acceptance, validation, affirmation, and approval are met. A child whose physical needs are met, in addition to receiving some recognition and acceptance, will feel and behave very differently from the child who is always hungry and abused.

When needs are met, a feeling of satisfaction follows. When needs are not met, the child's first inclination is to develop behaviors to protect against more hurt. Unmet needs hurt too much to stay open and vulnerable; distancing becomes a common protective mechanism. Distancing behaviors are learned early in life and are maintained in adulthood. Protection against hurt also means avoidance of ways of relating that are not hurtful; not believing comments that are supportive, encouraging, heartening, and hopeful.

## Conflict is a Predictable Way of Creating Emotional Distance for Self-Protection

At birth, you were totally dependent on significant adults to meet your needs. They were your physical lifeline and psychological mirror; both were necessary to meet your needs. As you gained mobility, language, and self-control, your physical dependency on your parents decreased, yet you still relied on them for many of your psychological needs. Are you dependent on significant adults in any way now? If so, if what ways? If not, when did you stop feeling dependent on them?

As a child you did not know (and neither did they) that your parents' responses to your needs were directly related to the degree of satisfaction of their childhood needs. Your parents could not give you what they did not have. An obvious example is when a child is hungry and his parent does not have any food, the feeling within the child is different from being hungry and receiving a full balanced meal.

Or when a child needs approval and her parent is lacking in self-approval, the child's needs for approval cannot be met. When needs are satisfied, the feelings and behavior are very different from unsatisfied needs. The nature of the need is not as primary as the satisfaction of the need. A need is a need.

Pre-language children are unable to verbalize to parents about their unmet needs. To state what you are needing is a skill that many adults struggle to learn who have a command of language. So much of what happens between parent and child is unspoken, is felt, and is acted out.

Young children, sensing the feelings of their internal discomfort and struggle (unmet needs), need to find ways of protecting themselves from more discomfort. Distance is a protective behavior; it is a predictable way of creating emotional and physical distance. When you stub your toe on a rock, your first inclination is to protect your toe and to either move or avoid the rock. When it is not possible to move the rock, avoidance is the next best coping behavior.

Distance is accompanied by certain thoughts that in turn help to maintain the distance. These thoughts develop from the child's perception and eventually become ingrained beliefs that regulate closeness and distance. The following example shows this process.

## Winston

Winston was the oldest of two sons born to parents who had immigrated from Europe two years after his birth. His parents struggled to learn the language and culture while finding a place for themselves in the United States. Both had experienced hardships in their native country and had many dreams for their sons: dreams of how they wished it could have been for them as children. Unknowingly and with the best of intentions, all of Winston's parents' dreams were projected onto him.

Winston, a quiet, pensive, and reserved person, needed and preferred quietude and privacy especially when he was studying and mastering a new task. His mother had a need to be with him, talk incessantly, and make sure "everything was well with him." Winston experienced his mother's behaviors as annoying, bothersome, and intrusive. It was as though she was forcing her dream to happen, all coming from her unmet needs.

As Winston got older, his need for privacy increased. He could not concentrate on his school work when his mother was constantly talking and interfering, yet he knew that his mother was well-intentioned. He employed many ways to let her know what he needed—talking to her, being helpful, working when she was involved in her own projects, and avoiding being at home when he had her permission to be gone. Nothing worked. His mother's fears and needs overshadowed his needs.

Only in his adulthood, as he has struggled with depression, has he realized that the only way that his mother would allow him his quietude and privacy was to depress. When he went into the cocoon of his depression, she left him alone. Depression provided the space and distance that he needed to do schoolwork and projects, read, or be quiet with himself.

The belief that he created—When I depress (go into a depression) my mother does not interfere—became a tightly woven cocoon that he is working hard to crawl out of and change to a new belief—I can say *no* to others and expect to be heard when I need privacy." Ironically, as an adult, his depression invites others to take care of him, which he will not allow, or to distance themselves from him.

Winston remembers the constant conflict when he needed some quiet and private time to simply complete his homework or spend time with his friends. As an adult, he can still hear his mother say, "Do you have your homework done yet? Can I help you with anything? Are you hungry? How much longer will it take until you are finished? You are so lucky to be in a country where you can get a good education. I didn't have that chance when I was young. Do your friends want to stay for dinner?"

Winston's mother believed that she could feel fulfillment through her son; his action would make her happy. Instead she did not meet a need that was very important to him and created intense conflict.

Conflict comes from what is going on inside you: your feelings, unmet needs, thoughts, ideas, beliefs, attitudes, perceptions, and reactions. It does not come from your child's behaviors.

## Conflict Does Not Come From Your Child's Behavior

A very popular belief is that conflict comes from your children's behavior, a belief that is the ultimate in teaching and enhancing victimization. Believing this idea puts you constantly at the mercy of what your children choose to do, leaving you feeling powerless and frustrated. Most of the time, your kids are just simply being kids. Normal, ordinary, regular, typical, and usual kids. They are twenty or thirty years younger than you whom you love and who love you. They have no intention of creating turmoil or discomfort for you. If this is your belief, you learned it when your parents told you in direct and subtle ways that you were the cause of the conflict between them and you. You continue to perpetuate the myth.

You no doubt remember the times such as the morning when you awoke feeling grumpy and out-of-sorts. Your socks would not go on your feet straight and you spilled your glass of orange juice at breakfast and were blamed for making your mother or father late for work. You were being a kid: needing comfort, room to be a kid, and understanding and forgiveness for your spill. Your mother or father, in the rush of the morning, did not allow the time that you needed to be a kid with all of the accompanying behaviors. Instead, each felt frustrated and reacted to you, saying that you were the cause of how each was inconvenienced. At times, parents forget to allow time for the unexpected.

Conflict that happens between you and your child comes from your perception of and the meaning that you give to what is happening at the moment. A parent once told me that life is ten percent what happens and ninety percent how you react. Your reactions were learned from your varied life experiences to date, how you felt inside at that time, and the conclusions, beliefs, and attitudes that became a part of your thinking. The example of Julianne portrays how conflict does not come from children's behavior and intensifies when either participant is not acknowledging his/her part of the interaction.

## Julianne

Julianne was an obedient child during elementary and middle school. She felt an obligation as an only child to make her parents proud of her. She was an honor student and was active in sports, school, and community activities. Since turning seventeen and beginning her senior year, she felt a need for more freedom and independence. Her parents, especially her mother, were very close to her and were having trouble letting her go. They wanted to keep on protecting her, making her decisions for her, monitoring her activities, and choosing her friends.

Julianne, like all seventeen-year-olds, needed more freedom and control over her life. She knew that in a year she would be away at college, needing to be self-reliant. She needed the opportunity to practice her self-reliance in the safety of her home. If she made mistakes, she hoped that her family would be more gracious and forgiving than people she would encounter outside the family. What she was asking for was reasonable and age-appropriate.

Julianne was needing more freedom. Her parents, especially her mother, needed to keep on mothering her and to keep Julianne their good little girl who was dependent on them. Julianne felt much resentment for their lack of acceptance of her age and what she needed. Julianne acted out her resentment in several ways.

She became very secretive and private; she would not give her parents details of where she was going, with whom she was, or what she did as she had done when she was a younger child. She also gained independence by rejecting the friends her parents selected for her and instead chose her own friends. In these two ways, as she resisted her parents' control, did she express her resentment and feel the freedom that was her entitlement.

Julianne knew that she used good judgment and could take care of herself just as she had learned to do when she was a younger child. She also knew that her behavior made perfect sense, given her age and need for independence.

Conversely, Julianne's parents, struggling to let their daughter go and alarmed at their daughter's independent behaviors, were in constant conflict with her. They accused Julianne of not loving them anymore and accused her friends of changing her into a bad girl, a gross exaggeration. They accused Julianne of making terrible mistakes that she would blame on her parents and would live with regrets for the rest of her life. The extent that parents go to stay in control!

The first time that we talked, Julianne's parents let me know very clearly that their daughter's behavior was the cause of the conflict. Her mother said, "Our only daughter is causing us such turmoil. She is ruining our lives. She is a good girl turned bad. We don't know what got into her. She is running with the wrong crowd and we are devastated." They rejected Julianne's behavior and chose to feel devastated. In contrast, they liked the actions of the younger, perfect, obedient Julianne who did everything that she was told. It was obvious that they were personalizing Julianne's behavior, that is, interpreting her actions as statements about them as parents, rather than Julianne's developmental tasks.

Your believing that the conflict between you and your child is all about your child's actions leads to your overlooking important details; your corresponding reaction is exaggerated and not rational.

Julianne's parents' inner struggle was to let go of their need to control her life, to look beyond Julianne's behavior and to understand what she needed to do. With these acknowledgments, they could support her independence and decrease the conflict between them. No easy task. Julianne's parents did not have a semester course in "Parenting 101: How to Graciously Let Go of Your Child." They needed Julianne for their sense of fulfillment and expected her to behave as she did in grade school.

Julianne's parents worked hard to see and accept what was happening within each of them and to let go of their wonderful daughter. Months later her mother reframed her response in the following self-respecting way:

"My only child is grown-up. I am not ready for her to leave me. I have loved mothering her and have felt such satisfaction and fulfillment. She is a good person. I am a good person. I am in a huge life transition and choose to take more control over my life and less control over Julianne's life. I need to find something in my life that will be a source of satisfaction and fulfillment for me. That is my responsibility.

"I need to mourn my loss and shift my focus to viewing her as a peer. My daughter is grown and does not need me like she did as a young child. No one ever told me how difficult it would be when my baby grew-up. If I had been told, I would not have believed them. I need experience to understand. I now have that experience."

Conflict within you and between you and your child is all about unmet needs or unfulfilled expectations, not badness.

There are no bad people, only people who believe they are bad.

## Conflict is Learned and Comes From Unmet Needs or Unfulfilled Expectations

Each time you experienced conflict as an infant and young child, you felt a specific feeling of distress. The feeling came from a need that you had that was dependent on adult assistance to be met. When the situation was repeated frequently, you felt the same feelings. You did not say to yourself, "Oh well, my need did not get met. It's OK. No big deal. Maybe the next time I will experience the satisfaction that I deserve." Only as an adult can you learn to be that accepting and forgiving.

Instead, you developed certain beliefs about yourself that you carry into your adulthood and parenting as a way of coping, surviving, and dealing with your feelings from your unmet needs. Some situations created conflict upon conflict for you. The following examples show this process.

I know a mother who is very dedicated and available to help people in the community who have had surgery, extended illnesses or hardships, and have needs that require assistance from another person. She has received awards and recognition from local service groups for her outstanding altruism.

Her twelve-year-old daughter Hannah has modeled her mother's helpfulness and periodically needs time with her mother to talk and share about her day. Her mother is so busy responding to others' needs that she is unavailable to her daughter. The gifts of time, support, understanding, caring, empathy, and love that her mother gives so freely to others get used up by the time she is home with her family.

Hannah admires her mother's assistance to others, knows her caring for people in need is wonderful, copies the same behavior in her relationships, yet she feels left out. She needs time with her mother. Hannah's inner conflict is intensified because "How can I justify feeling upset at my mother who is a good Samaritan to others? My needs to be listened and responded to are as great as other peoples' needs for caring. After all, I am her daughter."

When Hannah's mother was a young child many of her needs for recognition, approval, affirmation, and closeness were not met. The way that she chose to manage her resultant feelings was to do for others what she wanted done for herself. The behavior that she selected was a way of coping with and compensating for the pain that she felt. Her behavior became a way of life for her, and as ironic as it sounds, kept her from responding to her daughter's needs. History, that powerful force, once again is repeated.

Hannah developed the belief, "I am not as important to my mother as are other people." Her greatest struggle was knowing what to do with her feelings of exclusion, knowing that she could not be angry directly at a mother who was so comforting and helpful to so many people.

Needs that are not met for very young children can create a conflictive relationship for many years unless the unmet need is identified, met, and discussed. This was true for Timothy.

Timothy was one year old when his mother became very sick and was unable to care for him for the next three years. She spent those years in and out of hospitals with the in-between times at home unable to meet his many needs. Although he had many caretakers who were kind and responsive to him, he keenly felt his mother's absence.

When Timothy was four, his mother's recovery was complete enough for her to take charge of his total care. For three years, Timothy had felt a deep loss and was able at age five to verbalize, "My heart is aching." Both he and his mother had missed three very critical years; for Timothy it was the years of significant motor and speech development, gaining his first sense of himself, and declaring his continually emerging independence. For his mother it meant giving her attention, time, and energy to recovering her physical and emotional health and not being active in Timothy's development. The three years was a loss for each of them. Yet, as the fourth ground rule says, *At any time I am doing the best I can do;* both Timothy and his mother were doing their best.

To compensate for the lack of consistency with numerous caregivers and the loss that Timothy felt, he told himself that he needed to be in charge of the situation and consequently, developed many behaviors that could be described as controlling and bossy. He told himself that he was at risk and had to be in charge of the situation, a huge task for a little boy. His need was to have his mother available to share with him, meet his needs, and be in charge of the situation.

In another situation, Donna's need came from her delayed language development and feelings of frustration when others did not understand her. She was three years old and could not speak clearly enough to be understood. As she struggled one day to communicate with her mother about a need, her frustration intensified to the point of screaming in garbled words, "Just forget it." Her mother felt equally frustrated and buried her hurt inside, listening so carefully to hear what her daughter could not say.

After many years of intensive speech and language therapy, Donna's speech was articulate. Yet the same feelings of frustration and hopelessness were inside her. Her belief is that others do not understand what she says, so forget about talking and explaining. Her approach to many tasks that do not go well at the beginning is "Just forget it."

The example of Jordon shows how unmet needs create and fuel conflicts that last for many years.

Jordon was three when his parents were fighting verbally and physically. Jordon awakened from his nap and came into the living room. Both parents were out-of-control with rage and fear. Jordon's mother was heckling his father who had reached the limit of his anger. At that moment, Jordon's mother picked him up just as his father swung his fist at her. Mother, still holding Jordan swung her other fist at his father and screamed loudly. Jordan, frightened and the only one in control, screamed to his mother, "Mommy, get out of here." His mother came to her senses and left the house.

Jordon continued to be in control of the situation and relationship with his mother as he attempted to comfort his mother who was feeling ashamed of how she had lost control. Jordon became his mother's emotional caretaker, a role that was beyond his age, wisdom, skill, and maturity level, and a role that he maintained until age eleven when his mother slowly regained her role as the adult in their relationship.

Jordan's need was to feel safe, protected, and cared for by both parents. His experience during this critical incident gave him control and power that he continued to demand for many years. His mother found herself feeling frightened of his reaction, especially when she said *no* to him. When Jordon heard a *no*, he immediately found a way to make his mother say *yes*. Mother, attempting to avoid more conflict, frequently changed her *no* to *yes*. Jordon's need to have his parent be in charge again was not met. His mother, feeling her fear and shame, tells herself that she is the adult in charge. Her thoughts are the opposite of how she was feeling.

## How You Think May Be
## Different From How You Feel

In order to survive the conflict that you felt as a child, it was necessary to say something to yourself that made some sense and justified the feelings at that moment. It is too scary for a child to say how she is feeling, knowing the adult is not meeting her needs. That level of honesty may feel threatening to the adult, and children are aware of the times when adults feel threatened and defensive. In the earlier example, Hannah missed her mother's time and attention while her mother was responding to other people's needs in the community. Since Hannah knew that her mother's efforts were kind, it was difficult for her to feel anger and sadness about her unmet needs.

The conclusion that Hannah drew about her situation "I am not as important as other people or my mother would tend to me first," led to another conclusion that became a guide for her behavior:

If I am good to others, they'll be good to me and my needs will get met. The first conclusion allowed her to tolerate the pain that she felt, and the second conclusion helped her to compensate for the pain. How she felt was different from what she thought which was different from how she acted. These might be the same conclusions Hannah's mother believed.

Timothy, whose mother was ill for three years, concluded that he needed to be in charge and compensated with the belief that he knew everything about everything. He felt unsure about himself, yet kept thinking that he knew it all.

Donna, who struggled to speak clearly, concluded: No one ever listens to me and compensated by withdrawing. Her feelings of frustration were covered by her quiet withdrawal.

Frequently thought conclusions become beliefs. Beliefs, in turn, create feelings that create behaviors. And it all starts with a child's need that was not satisfied. The feelings may be different from the thought; the thought justifies the feelings; action and behaviors compensate for the feelings. To decrease conflict it is necessary to understand this cycle of conflict.

## How to Decrease Conflict

The obvious way to decrease conflict between you and your child is to understand what and whose needs are screaming to be met. Easier said than done. The following seven steps can lessen the conflicts.

(1) It is necessary to want and to imagine fewer conflicts. When I ask a father if he can picture fewer conflicts between him and his daughter and he says, "No," I hear that the pattern of turmoil is so ingrained that change is very difficult. Picturing how it can be different helps you to move from where you are to another way of relating. The difference is an attitude of hopelessness versus hopefulness.

(2) It is necessary for you to step back far enough to see the whole picture. This includes the setting, what is going on in you, what is going on in your child, and what is still unresolved from past conflicts. The following is a common scene. You come home from shopping, hoping that your son has mowed the lawn, and

instead find him shooting baskets with his best friend. You yell at him and accuse him of being lazy and uncaring about the family. Then you realize that you had casually mentioned your need to have the lawn mowed two days earlier and the warm sunshine of the first spring day made your son think of basketball rather than cutting the grass. Your son's reaction from your accusation is different from his reaction when you give him a respectful reminder.

(3) Understand that the content (what is being fought about) may have very little relevance to the conflict. You have experienced those conflicts where after the tensions have subsided that you forget what the conflict was about. The content had very little to do with the fight. The conflict was about something more important and less evident at the time—an unmet need or unfulfilled expectation.

(4) Know, as emphasized in this chapter, that the conflict does not come from your child's behavior. Rather it comes from your reaction to your child's actions. You are in control of your reactions, not your child's behavior. By focusing on your child's behavior, you tend to personalize what your child is doing which is more about what is going on inside your child than you. *Each time I speak, I really am saying more about myself than I am saying about you, even though I attach your name to it.*

(5) Accept and value yourself enough to discuss the conflict with your child in a respectful and peaceful manner. Your integrity, self-esteem, and personal boundaries are key and allow you to dialogue with your children in an open manner to affect more understanding, love, and mutual respect.

(6) Allow yourself to feel whatever pain you remember from your childhood. Acknowledge the needs that did not get met. Move through, rather than deny, the pain as a sure way of healing, then feeling, and gaining your own emotional freedom.

(7) As the conflict is decreased between you and your child, give yourself and your child credit for the changes. Never take changes for granted. They are cause for praise and celebration. Both promote healing.

→ **For Your Journal**

Be very specific as you answer the following questions. With which child do you experience the most conflict? What is the content of the conflict? Do some situations create more conflict than others? What unmet needs from your childhood create conflict in your relationships with your children? What have you done to heal those hurts and meet those needs? How often do you sit down with your children and ask each of them how they are feeling to get a sense of what needs might want to be met?

Use the seven steps to decrease conflict and write down your thoughts and reflections about the process. Share your thoughts with your children.

→ **Remember . . .**

- As a child, you focused on and were dependent on the reactions and responses of your parents. They were your lifeline and mirror; both were necessary for your survival.

- You did not know that your parents' responses to you were a statement of their fulfilled or unmet needs.

- Needs that are met result in contentment and satisfaction.

- Shift your focus from your child's behavior to your reaction and you decrease conflict.

- Adults who enter parenthood with their needs met, feel fulfilled and have more time, energy, and support to give to their children.

- See the kid in your children and allow them room to be kids. Childhood is a short time.

## Chapter 12 Overview

## Parent Stress and Burnout

- Your Most Demanding Job Has the Potential for Stress and Burnout
- The Demands Will Always be Greater Than your Energy
- Stress Comes From Your Reactions to Your Chilldren, Not Their Behaviors
- What You Say and Do When You are Rested is Different From When You are Exhausted and Stressed
- You Care for Yourself to the Degree That You Believe You are a Very Important Person (VIP)
- How to Prevent Stress and Burnout
- For Your Journal
- Remember . . .

# 12

## Parent Stress and Burnout

### Parent stress and burnout:

- develop in your most demanding job in the universe and involve being on-the-job twenty-four hours a day, seven days a week, fifty-two weeks a year, for a total of at least twenty years.

- mean accepting that the demands and requests on you will always be greater than your physical and emotional energies. This was also true for your parents.

- occur in degrees. They come from your reactions to your children; they do not come from your children or their behaviors.

- involve knowing that statements made from a state of exhaustion and excess stress are different from those made from a state of restfulness and relaxation. The impact on your children is just as drastic.

- include your knowing about the direct relationship that exists between your belief about being a VIP (very important person) and how you take care of yourself. You get tired and need to learn to find ways to rejuvenate yourself on a regular basis. If not, your exhaustion creates unnecessary conflict and crises.

- entail the belief, "Only I can keep track of my energy levels. My kids are too busy being kids."

- include knowing that your children sense when you are exhausted. Be honest with yourself, or you will take your exhaustion out on your kids.

- are avoided when you know the following: (1) When you feel like you cannot take a break is probably the time you need it most, and (2) It is futile to say, "Give me a break." You need to find a way to take a break. Your kids cannot give it to you.

- are prevented by learning to say no directly without feeling guilty. Indirect nos create conflict and, in the long run, use more energy. Saying no at appropriate times allows your children the opportunity to become more responsible for themselves.

- are prevented by knowing deeply that children are geniuses at using guilt, comparisons, exaggerations, buttering-up, silence, temper-tantrums, and cries of "It's not fair" as forms of manipulation to get a yes when a no is stated.

- are prevented by choosing to focus on what you do rather than what you do not do; you see the glass as half-full, rather than half-empty.

- knowing how to avoid it, models for your children how to care for themselves.

## Your Most Demanding Job
## Has the Potential For Stress and Burnout

Parenting is exhausting! Your time and energy are spent doing, not thinking about, or assessing what degree of stress you are feeling. Rarely do you wake up in the morning thinking, "On a scale from one to ten, with ten being the highest, my stress level is at eight and a-half right now. Wow, I need to watch myself today, so I don't go over the edge and take my low energy out on my kids. I am in charge of taking care of me, and since my energy reserve is low, I also need to find ways to re-fuel myself today." If you have learned to gauge your energies, good for you!

Instead, you think of the long list of responsibilities that are on your schedule that day, hoping that you have the energy to complete them all. What might be left-over for you, if any, is an afterthought. Even when you say to yourself that you will have more time for yourself when your children are older, you find that as you get to that point what changes is the nature of the responsibilities. The time you spend responding to helping and meeting their needs is the same and sometimes more.

For instance, the difference is between watching your toddler play in the back yard and watching her play Little League Baseball when she is ten-years-old. She is counting on you to be there at both times. Both situations call for your time, concentration, and responsiveness. All take energy.

Parenting is unlike any other job because there is so much responsibility, for such a long time, and your actions have long-lasting impact on yourself and your children. Your job is twenty-four hours a day, seven days a week, fifty-two weeks a year, for at least twenty years. Your time and energy commitment is as monumental as the corresponding potential for stress and burnout. Unlike a seven-to-three or nine-to-five position, you are always on-line and on-call. You do not get one day off each week and three weeks paid vacation each year. The needs, wants, demands, and requests are always present calling for a response.

Responsiveness takes energy—constant and endless energy. Usually it is mental, versus physical, energy that includes switching from what you were thinking about at a given moment to what your child is asking. It includes getting the relevant information that you need, thinking about her question/request, and deciding what you believe is your best answer/decision.

Parents often tell me that it is easier to handle feeling worn out physically than mentally because the two kinds of fatigue are different. You can recover more quickly from physical tiredness than mental weariness by going to sleep. Letting go of your thoughts that seem to run constantly is not so easy.

The needs of very young children are more simple (food, rest, shelter, safety, protection) and, therefore, easier to meet. In addition, young children have not yet learned how to challenge and manipulate you and your decisions. As your children get older, have their own vocabulary and use of words, and make more sophisticated demands, defining your responses can be more challenging and time-consuming. Be aware that kids frequently tell you that if you do not give them the answer they want to hear, you do not love them. This common threat and manipulation tears at the core of your heart since one thing you are sure about in parenting (most of the time) is that you love your children.

An example of this is a first-grader who asked for a very expensive electronic game for his birthday. His parents knew that it was too costly for their limited budget and, in addition, they had some concerns about the game being a passing fad. His parents spent considerable time discussing their son's selection, agreed that it was not a good idea, and chose a gift that was within their budget that would last for several years. Their son was so intent on getting the game that his initial reaction was one of disappointment and he accused them of not loving him.

Fortunately, his parents had enough self-respect to not personalize their son's first response and accusation. The son confused love with his parents' saying *yes*. His parents knew that what love had to do with the situation was the careful way in which they listened and gave careful consideration to his wish, the gift they selected (that in time became his favorite), and how they remained adult and self-regarding throughout the entire time.

Be clear that your income, time, energy level, and saying *yes* have nothing to do with love. Confusing these only takes mental energy that you need constantly. If you are confusing these, separate them now.

You as a parent never have an infinite amount of experience, maturity, energy, skill, or wisdom to respond to the constant requests of your children, especially at the precise moment of the need. The same goes for any adults who are child caretakers. You are human. You get tired, exhausted, cranky, and irritable. You have your limits. You are a candidate for stress and burnout. Parenting is all-encompassing and never-ending. The task is never done or complete. There is never enough of you to do all that needs to be done.

## The Demands Will Always be Greater Than Your Energy

Taking into account your children's ages, your age, and energy levels, your children's requests and demands exceed your available time and energy. Do you ever, as you are falling asleep at night, feel that during the day you completed everything that you wanted to do for yourself and your children? This includes physical and psychological caring for yourself, listening and responding in a focused, respectful and peaceful manner to your children's needs and requests, maintaining your adult relationships, and accomplishing the necessary household chores.

Then, as you feel wonderful about your day, you let go into a deep, restful sleep, and wake up in the morning, ready for and anticipating a great day. If that happens, you have learned how to deal with the stressors uncertainties, challenges, obstacles that look impossible, demands, requests, and tensions in parenting. Good for you!

More likely, your thoughts include what you did not accomplish today and what and how today's events and incidents occurred. Your thoughts also include your schedule for tomorrow and how you want tomorrow to be different from today.

For just one day, mark down every time you respond to a need, question, demand, or request from your children. This includes and is not limited to: feeding, changing, bathing, and holding your infant; dressing your twenty-month-old who is on the brink of her first sense of independence; saying *no* many times to your two-year-old as he climbs on top of the desk, and you reach quickly to catch him from falling; answering a curious why question (the twentieth one of the morning) from your four-year-old whose questions start when she awakens and ends as she falls asleep; taking your five-year-old and the cupcakes you baked for his birthday to preschool; grocery shopping with three kids; buying clothes for your seven-year-old who wants everything in the store except what you went to buy; attending a parent-teacher conference for your ten-year-old; sewing a ripped seam in your twelve-year-old son's jeans; doing laundry, an endless, thankless task; preparing for your fourteen-year-old's sleep-over birthday party; taking your fifteen-year-old driving; listening to your sixteen-year-old share her distress about her relationships; and attending your eighteen-year-old's graduation.

The list goes on and on. This is not overlooking the fights you survive, encouragement and support you give to all family members, slivers you remove from fingers, telephone calls, "ouchies" you heal, stories you read, bikes you repair, meals you prepare, trips to the doctor's office, muddy shoes you clean, budgets you balance, and school field trips you chaperon. You do so much; all of it is important and is your response to your children's continuous needs. No wonder you get tired!

Simply stated, there is never enough of you to go around; the twenty-four hours in your day and seven days in your week seem inadequate. You wish for extra moments that never come. Wishing neither conserves nor increases your energy and is as magical as giving your power to your children by believing that they create your tensions. Instead, you are in charge of your stress which comes from your reactions to your children's behaviors.

## Stress Comes From Your Reactions to Your Children, Not Their Behavior

Your children do not create your stress; your reactions to your children and their actions create your stress. This opposes a popular belief that is continually reinforced with the following statements from parents:

- My son gives me grey hair.

- My daughter took two years off of my life.

- He gets me so upset and stressed out.

- She makes me so mad and makes me lose control.

- I am calm and collected, and then, just like that, she sets me off.

- He gives me headaches.

- I walk around on eggshells all the time with my oldest son.

- I can't relax with my kids around.

- My kids drive me up the wall and give me ulcers.

- My daughter makes my life miserable.
- I don't think I'll survive my kids.
- My kids are my life. I live for them.

These comments perpetuate the myth that your stress comes from your children rather than your attitude toward and reaction to them and what they do. It is much easier to say that your child causes you to feel a certain way than to take ownership for your reaction to your child's actions. In fact, as intense, harsh, or disrespectful as your child's behavior is, your reaction to her behavior is all that you control. The more you struggle to understand and incorporate this idea into your thinking, the more freedom you feel, and the less stress you create.

Of equal challenge is knowing that your feelings at a given moment and the state that you are in (tense, relaxed, scared, happy) affect and color your perceptions, reactions, and responses. When you are feeling relaxed and peaceful, what you see looks peaceful and your response is the same. When you are feeling edgy and tense, your responses come from those same feelings.

Mild levels of stress are necessary for you to stay alert and attentive to a task. Mild levels of stress are just enough mental and body tension to sustain your focus and concentration. Excessive stress levels are too much mental and body tension that interfere with your focus and concentration. Excessive stress over long periods of time is debilitating, and leads to burnout and physical and psychological illnesses and disorders.

There are two kinds of stressors, external and internal. External stressors are outside of you and your control while internal stressors are within you and are in your control. Your children and their behaviors are an example of an external stressor, and your attitude and reaction toward your children and their behaviors are an example of an internal stressor.

By not understanding the distinction between these two kinds of stressors, you most likely assume that your children and their behaviors cause your tension, and if and when they change themselves and their actions, then you will feel more relaxed and calm. This puts too much responsibility on your children for how you are feeling. They have enough to do learning who they are and how to value and take care of themselves.

Economizing your energy levels, decreasing your stress, and avoiding burnout are choices that you have, choices that necessitate a radical shift in your thinking. This change from focusing on your children's behavior to your thinking characterizes what you control. See pages 55, 56, and 57 for the list of what you as parents control and do not control. Your thinking and your reactions are totally in your control.

You are never in control of another person's behavior, not even your children's. Your children have their own minds and lives. Believing that you are in control of your children's behavior leaves you continually feeling upset, frustrated, and angry when they do not do what you want them to do. Your frustration, in turn, creates undue and excessive stress.

When you are feeling in control of yourself, your need to control what is outside of you is lessened. You are more peaceful. When you are feeling rested and relaxed, your behavior is different from when you are feeling tense and stressed. You are more peaceful and so are your responses.

## What You Say and Do When You Are Rested is Different From When You Are Exhausted and Stressed

How are you different when you are rested and relaxed from when you are exhausted and stressed? You certainly know this difference in your children and go to great lengths to avoid their getting overly-tired. You are also keenly aware of how you and your children feel when you are on vacation and away from the usual routine and stressors.

Parents often share with me how the decreased stress levels of vacation create joyful times with less irritability and friction, more patience and cooperation, sustained periods of humor and lightness, and heightened creativity and closeness. How short-lived the benefits of vacation are when you return to your usual and routine schedule! Looking back to your vacation, you remember the tranquility.

Exhaustion and tenseness are more readily identified after the fact. For instance, you have had a very busy, exhausting week and it is finally (or too quickly) Friday evening. You are dog-tired; all you want to do is get everyone in bed and go to sleep yourself. Your teenager wants to have two friends sleep over, your eleven-year-old is excited about finishing a science project for school and is asking for your assistance, and your nine-year-old wants you to go shopping for items for her birthday party that is two weeks away. You yell at your teenager about how selfish she is to think only about her needs and not yours, you snap at your eleven-year-old for not working on his project during the week, and you threaten your nine-year-old with not having a birthday party if she is going to be so demanding. When you do fall into bed, collapse into sleep, and awaken in the morning, you feel bad about how you yelled at or threatened your children. You apologize to them, acknowledging how tired you were, and now, feeling more rested, you feel less stressed.

In other words, frequently you are not aware of how tired or exhausted you are until you get some rest or spend time alone and feel the contrast. Looking back, feeling more rested and less stressed, the situation looks different. Not only do you realize how stressed you were, you remember how your tenseness got projected onto your children with responses full of irritability, exaggerations, and impatience.

Rather than feeling bad or guilty, which might be your first reaction, use your awareness to help you keep track of your energy levels. And remember, energy and love are two individual issues. Keep them separate. Retrospection is a wonderful tool if you use it for, not against, yourself. This compares with your belief about your importance and value and how you take care of yourself.

## You Care For Yourself to the Degree that You Believe You Are a Very Important Person (VIP)

As in all other aspects of parenting, your beliefs about yourself affect what you do for yourself and your children. Your response to and treatment of people, possessions, and events in your life that are important to you are different from ones less significant. What and who you value, you treat in different ways from what and who you do not value.

How do you prepare for and respond to someone who you believe is very important? At work, you might go out of your way to make arrangements for a visit from an off-site supervisor, auditor, consultant, or district manager. At home, anticipating your favorite uncle's visit might motivate you to take time to finish an overdue project, rearrange some household items, or clean the garage that has five years of clutter. In other words, you expend energies doing extras that you do not do routinely.

With your valued possessions, (photographs, china, crystal, collectibles, heirlooms, and important documents) you take special care to avoid damage or destruction. With your financial investments, you stay current and informed of interest rates and other opportunities to increase and secure your monies. You take measures to protect your cherished possessions.

Important events that mark life milestones, herald accomplishments, and signal major transitions like births, birthdays, weddings, anniversaries, job promotions, graduations, and retirements are frequently planned for well in advance. You pay much attention to details to ensure that the occasion goes well.

Like those significant people, possessions, and events, your time and energy are major investments in your child's life. Your energies are as valuable as you. Do you allow yourself to think about yourself in that way? If not, what is interfering? How you care for yourself has consequences for you now, the rest of your life, and what you model for your children. Parenting is for a long time and takes enormous amounts of energy.

Only you can keep track of your energy levels. Believing that you are a VIP to your children helps you to monitor your energies in addition to the following ways of economizing your energies.

## How to Prevent Stress and Burnout

Avoiding an accident is better than picking up the pieces and rebuilding. Preventing stress is better than recovering from burnout.

Parents tell me that they have too much to do; adding stress-prevention to their list adds to more overload. My response is "Can you afford to not think about your stressful events and stress levels?" Sometimes it takes that one moment of patience, forethought, or reflection to make a difference: the difference is between avoiding or preventing a spill, mishap, or mistake versus cleaning up the mess. The difference starts with how you are feeling and ends up enhancing or detracting from your peacefulness.

The following are ways to monitor, avoid, prevent, and decrease your stress levels.

**Watch your energy gauge.** What you monitor will not sneak up on you. This involves your taking time periodically to think about how much energy you have. Think of it as your energy barometer and accept wherever it is at that moment. Like other barometers, there is fluctuation depending on you and your children's needs. If you are recovering from an illness, injury, or trauma and your daughter's best friend dies, the balance between what you have to give and what she needs is precarious.

At these times, be honest with what you have to give, knowing it is acceptable, honest, and human to acknowledge your limitations. Having limitations with your energy has nothing to do with love. Your love for your children has no limitations. The alternative is not accepting your limitations, giving and then feeling resentful, and modeling dishonesty. A small gift given freely is better than a large gift given with resentment or bitterness. Your children know the difference.

If it is difficult for you to be honest and direct when you are exhausted. At such times you will no doubt fall into the trap of finding indirect ways of getting some space or privacy, even though you will have to deal with the effects of your indirectness. Some common ways are, ignoring others, picking fights and being mad, giving partial answers, and feigning illness; all behaviors that invite distance and, if you are prone toward guilt, provide you with something to feel guilty about.

**When you feel that you cannot take a break is the time you need it most.** Another parenting paradox! When you are exhausted, stretched, or stressed to the maximum is when you need a break and respite from your responsibilities. Those are the times when you feel least like you can afford a respite time. Difficult times are during extended recovery periods from sickness, accidents, and traumas, when you experience overload at work or in other areas of your life, and when you receive bad news about a loved one. These situations exaggerate both you and your child's needs with more demands put on your time and energies.

Children of all ages sense when you are exhausted or tense, and if you are not owning how you are feeling, you can count on them to act out their reactions to how they perceive you are feeling. Younger children get scared when they sense adults are not in control. Older kids either choose to be sensitive to you, behaving with cooperation and kindness, or take advantage of your perking on less than four burners by acting out in some way "to trigger you." Unwittingly, their behavior adds more energy, confusion, and complications to the situation, therefore, contributing to your stress levels.

I believe, in general, that children want to be sensitive and responsive to you if you will allow that to happen. This sensitivity is a common theme in my dialogues with children of all ages. Their sensitivity and responsiveness to you is not the same as their taking responsibility for you. Some parents believe that their honesty about their stress or fatigue puts responsibility on children; in fact, the opposite happens. Your openness and honesty say to your kids that you are monitoring your emotional and physical energy levels. Not being open and honest make kids wonder if you are keeping track for yourself and are fooling yourself. When you are honest with them in an open, direct, and nonmanipulative manner, your honesty creates a boundary for you and invites them to be responsive and cooperative. Each cooperative interaction decreases stress.

Children as young as three and four have the ability to be sensitive to you when you say, "I am not feeling well today, and I need you to listen to me and do what I say. I know that you can help me in that way. You are my wonderful helper." In this way, you facilitate the growth of your child's sense of kindness and empathy. Make sure to reinforce in a simple and genuine way behaviors that are self-respecting with a reply of, "Thank you for listening to me and doing what I said. You are a wonderful son/daughter. I am so fortunate to have you."

Taking a break, even a brief one, gives you renewed energies to deal with the situation. Sometimes that respite can be as short as reading for a few minutes; sitting, resting and paying close attention to your breathing; calling and talking with a friend; or taking a vacation in your mind by thinking of an earlier time when your situation was more relaxed and peaceful. Your memory is so wonderful (if you believe it is) and can help during stressful times even though the brief reprieve will always be less than what you want, need, or deserve.

**Know that it is futile to say to your kids, "Give me a break."** That is your responsibility and your children cannot give you that permission. It is not because they do not love you. It has nothing to do with love. It is more about him/her being a kid with dependency, wants, and narcissism that goes with the territory.

Give yourself permission to take necessary breaks. Often that means planning ahead to arrange child care for young children or leaving instructions for older children. Or it might entail your letting go of unfinished tasks. Parents tell me they will take time off when the kids are old enough, after the kitchen is clean, or when things settle down. There is never a convenient time. The job is too big.

**Learn to say _no_ directly without feeling guilty.** Indirect _nos_ create confusion for your children and take your energy. You might feel caught between wanting to say _yes_ and not having the energy to do what the _yes_ entails, so you feel ambivalent. Or you might have other thoughts on your mind and need time to switch gears and think about what you want your answer to be. Sitting on the fence, you give a weak _yes_ by saying, "I guess I can do that, I'll try to finish your . . ., I suppose so, Well O.K., Perhaps, I'll see, or Maybe."

Because most children want to hear a _yes_, they assume an affirmative response. Later when you realize that you cannot follow through on your ambivalent answer or indirect _no_ and you tell your child, you frequently get responses of "You said you would, You lied, That's not fair, or I hate you." It is their protestation of your indirectness and a bid for you to change your _no_ to _yes_.

You receive so many requests and questions daily from your children and you respond as often. Some answers are easy and obvious to you, and some take some deliberation for you to respond confidently. It is self-respecting to allow yourself time to think before you answer. You can respond with "I need some time to think about that and will let you know what my answer is, I need to discuss this with your mother (or father) and then I will give you an answer, I have too many things on my mind right now to think about that, or What you asked me is so important that I need to give it some careful thought. I will give you my answer soon."

Taking a reasonable amount of time to reflect on your response and not getting caught in your child's impatience for an answer now (when it can wait) helps you to reply with more confidence. Your yeses are a direct *yes* and your nos are a direct *no*. Even with your direct *no*, children can be geniuses at using the following forms of manipulation to get their way.

- Guilt responses, such as, "You never do anything for me, You don't care, (confusing love and saying *yes* and *no*), Jennifer's mom is nicer than you (using comparisons), I am the only person who cannot go (using exaggerations), You don't understand, and You were born in the Dark Ages." Guilt can tap into any feelings of inadequacy that you have, causing you to waver and doubt yourself.

- Buttering-up actions, such as, doing extra favors for you or begging p-lll-ease with all kinds of promises: "I'll keep my room clean, I'll be kind to my little brother, I'll listen to you, or I'll wake up the first time you call me." Make sure that you know when kindness is genuine or manipulative.

- Going silent and pouting as if saying maybe this will get to you and you will change your mind.

- Temper-tantrums that say see if my being out-of-control will scare you and make you change your mind?

- Screams of "That's not fair." Every parent wants to believe he/she is being fair and just, so this is a common one to trip you up. A self-respecting reply is, "You are right; it is not fair. Life is not fair. And my answer is still, *no*."

Be honest with where you are and keep it simple. If you are certain that your answer is *no*, say so directly and stick with it. Your children might not like it at the time, yet it is clear. Life has many *nos* and children need to learn that lesson. Practice being clear and direct and sticking to your response, if this is a difficult area for you.

**Learn to focus on and give yourself credit for what you do rather than what you do not do or get done.** Look at the glass being half-full, not half-empty. Crediting your strengths is a way of energizing yourself in addition to enhancing your self-esteem.

Use humor, telling yourself that you will probably survive your children's childhood and your kids will make it in spite of you.

Identify your external stressors, your children's behaviors, that tend to be difficult to deal with or seem to trigger a response in you that is less than self-respecting. Then identify your internal stressors, your perceptions of and reactions to the external stressors. What is it that you say to yourself? Do you think thoughts that are a personalization of what your child did, such as, "I know you did that on purpose, or You're out to get me?" Find another way of viewing the same behavior and creating a different response that is self-respecting. For example:

Your five-year-old dawdles at mealtime, taking what feels like forever to eat. All other family members have eaten their meals, are ready to leave the table, and there he is, dawdling. You pride yourself in your ability to organize and complete tasks in a reasonable amount of time. You hate dawdling (external stressor). It drives you nuts and your blood pressure skyrockets at mealtime (internal stressor, that is, your reaction to the external stressor). At the end of each meal, you find yourself getting upset, yelling at your son, vacillating between letting him sit by himself until he is finished eating to taking his food away and telling him that he cannot have anything to eat until the next meal. Your dislike of dawdling and your reaction create your stress and reinforce your child's behavior.

Any predictable scenario with predictable responses fortifies the same actions. You know that your son will dawdle, you hate dawdling, you have the same reaction, and your son responds in a familiar manner. At the next mealtime, the pattern repeats.

Viewing or reframing your child's dawdling behaviors in another way can decrease your stress levels and provide a more relaxed atmosphere at mealtime along with the potential for helping to change your son's behavior. Ways of reframing dawdling are the following: He sure knows how to pace himself, He eats so slowly that his food has time to digest, He is not a candidate for an ulcer, or He might as well enjoy the luxury of long, slow mealtimes now because he might not have that option as an adult. You can see how your response to any of these would be much different from what is familiar, creating lower levels of stress for you and your son.

**Remember that taking care of yourself is modeling the same for your children. They copy and imitate what you do.**

Allow and plan for regular breaks for yourself, knowing that you deserve to take good care of the most important adult male or female in your child's life—you. When your children are very young, you might choose to get up a half-hour earlier to have a few precious moments for yourself.

→ **For Your Journal**

Be specific as you think about, answer, and record the following questions.

1. What is stressful for you and what in your parenting takes the most energy? Is there something different that is stressful or relaxing in your relationship with each child?

2. How do you monitor your energy and stress levels? Are you in control of them or are they in control of you? How do you behave when you are exhausted or stressed?

3. How do you refill your energy tank when it is low? How do you relax and rejuvenate?

4. Do you believe that your reaction to your children's behavior, not their actions, create your tension? If yes, how do you keep track of your reactions? If no, would you be willing to entertain experimenting with this belief for several weeks? When you realize that you are feeling stressed, exhausted, or on overload, shift your focus from your children's behavior to what is going on inside you. Pay close attention to what you are saying to yourself and your reactions. Be creative as you see how you can reframe the

behaviors that you perceive to create stress in you?
The following are some examples that might be helpful.

## Change:

- FROM: Her constant questions drive me nuts.
  TO: She is a budding intellectual genius.

- FROM: He can't sit still for one second and he makes me so
  nervous.
  TO: He certainly is not a couch potato and no grass will ever
  grow under him. He does not have to worry about getting
  enough exercise.

- FROM: She gives me a hard time each morning when I awaken
  her. She never wants to get up.
  TO: Her behavior is constant and predictable each morning.
  I am never surprised at her morning behavior.

- FROM: He constantly reminds me of commitments that I've
  made to him. I can't get by with anything!
  TO: He has a perfect memory, even down to the last details.

- FROM: She argues with me all the time to the point that I
  feel stupid.
  TO: She sure is getting some great practice being a lawyer.
  No one will ever sell her anything that she does not want.

- FROM: He keeps everything inside to the point that I never
  know what he is thinking. It drives me wild!
  TO: I never have to worry about his keeping a secret.

- FROM: Her constant sticking her nose in everyone's business
  makes me crazy.
  TO: She is so alert and vigilant. She does not miss anything.
  She is like a watchdog.

- FROM: He has a one-track mind. It is so upsetting when I want
  to talk to him.
  TO: He has incredible powers of concentration.

- FROM: I climb the wall every time she does the opposite of
  what I tell her to do.
  TO: When she goes to school, she won't have to learn the
  definition of the word opposite. She already knows it well.

→ **Remember . . .**

- Your parenting job is never done. You need to take time to relax and take care of yourself.

- Parenting is your most significant job in energy output, long-term commitment, and influence.

- The stressors in parenting are as varied as the responsibilities. At times, responsibilities are stressors and vice versa.

- Your love for your children and their love for you are separate from the responsibilities that you have. Focusing on your love and not the responsibility is a source of energy.

- Be mindful of the many requests that you respond to in a given day and you will better understand your fatigue.

- Only you control your reactions to your children's actions. Knowing that your experience belongs to you decreases your internal stress levels.

- Mini-breaks and pauses can extend your energy. Remember that you are a VIP (very important person) to your children.

- Your children need you for a long time. Take care of yourself.

- You deserve and create your own peacefulness.

# Gifts
# Parents Give to
# Their Children

You are not aware of the many daily and life-long gifts that you give to your children. You may think of some of them as stressors, burdens, and responsibilities. Challenge yourself to view them as gifts that you give. Add to the list as you identify other gifts.

- Gift of life and genetic endowment. If it were not for you, your child would not be here.
- Gift of being his/her mother or father. Every child needs parents.
- Gift of time. The time you give is from your life and is considerable.
- Gift of energy. Children take much energy even at times when you feel as though you have none.
- Gift of sensitivity. You and your children are tender and sensitive.
- Gift of listening. You listen to what is and is not said.
- Gift of wisdom. Your wisdom comes from your experience with living.
- Gift of all of your learned skills. You have learned to cope emotionally, physically, socially, and spiritually.
- Gift of your knowledge. This includes all that you have learned in your lifetime.
- Gift of attention. You observe and consider your children's needs, desires, and wants.
- Gift of responsiveness. You respond in ways that meet your children's needs.
- Gift of patience. It takes a long time to parent and a long time for children to grow-up.
- Gift of your modeling and mentoring. How you feel and behave serves as a guide for your children.
- Gift of closeness. You are there during the difficult and pleasant times.

- Gift of warmth and comfort. These are most needed during the hurting and disappointing times.

- Gift of respect. You value and accept your children even when there are differences.

- Gift of abundance. You give them what you have especially your love.

- Gift of support. You are your child's cheerleader even when the team she is on is not winning.

- Gift of clearly defined limits. You know that your child learns self-discipline within the safety of limits.

- Gift of understanding, compassion, and empathy. You comprehend what your child is experiencing and know the accompanying feelings.

- Gift of loyalty. No one is as invested in your child as you.

- Gift of acceptance. This includes knowing who your child is and his strengths and weaknesses.

- Gift of discretion. You give discretion at the times when you separate who your wonderful child is from what he does and know what is and is not your issue.

- Gift of hope. Given what your child does and does not control and everything that your child has experienced, that she will grow up and be happy, self-respecting, responsible, and fulfilled.

- Gift of perseverance. Parenting is a minimum twenty year contract. That is a long time!

- Gift of letting go. From the letting go during the birthing process and through all of the developmental stages, you are constantly letting go. Some times are pleasant and some are painful. Your child is a separate person.

- Gift of challenging your child to be all that he can be. And your feeling jealous twinges of what you never got in your childhood.

- Gift of giving your children more opportunities than you had. Some opportunities come from the age you are living in and some from your own choices.

- Gift of loving yourself. This is your greatest gift; it is the essence of self-esteem and self-respect.

# Survival Kit For Parents

- Survival is knowing that you outlived your childhood and that fact is your best parenting resource.
- Survival is believing that your children grow up in spite of you.
- Survival is remembering the importance of self-esteem and integrity—first yours and then your child's.
- Survival is knowing that as you keep track of your child's developmental stages and accompanying tasks, your child's behavior makes more sense.
- Survival is remembering that the biggest difference between you and your children is twenty or thirty years, more joys, bumps and bruises, successes, disappointments, and more time to develop your life's philosophy and wisdom.
- Survival is developing patience as you wait for your children to grow up enough to appreciate you and thank you for all you gave. The average age range for this is from twenty to forty-five years.
- Survival is realizing that it is never too soon or too late to develop a warm, open, caring, and honest relationship with your children. Your children forgive your changes.
- Survival is knowing that you cannot make up through your children what you missed in your childhood.
- Survival is knowing that you create and maintain your own reality in your thinking. The same is true for your children.
- Survival is taking good care of yourself and reframing what you do not like.

# Epilogue

Parents are the unsung heros of the world. You have a tremendous responsibility teaching and training your children. You never feel adequate for the job and never get the recognition that is due you for your love, efforts, endurance, risking, learning, patience, and significance.

Your humanness continues to be your greatest asset and your greatest liability. You determine which asset or liability it is by how much you are believing in and loving yourself at any given moment.

Your challenge is to accept yourself and understand what you have experienced and how those experiences have influenced your life. Every interaction has some effect. The greater the importance of the person, the greater the impact.

The power inside you is greater than the power outside of you. Look within you before you look at your children.

Acknowledge your needs that were not met as a child and take charge now as an adult of meeting those needs.

Know that love is stronger than hate and fear.

See your child as a miracle for whom who you have the privilege of caring, learning to know and love, training and teaching, and letting go. Love yourself enough to say, "My child is so lucky to have me for his/her mom/dad."

May you continue to create much respect and peacefulness in your relationships with your children. That is what you and your children deserve.

# Books by Starburst Publishers

(Partial listing—full list available on request)

### *Parenting With Respect and Peacefulness*  —Louise A. Dietzel

Subtitled: *The Most Difficult Job in the World.* Parents who love and respect themselves parent with respect and peacefulness. Yet, parenting with respect is the most difficult job in the world. This book informs parents that respect and peace communicate love—creating an atmosphere for children to maximize their development as they feel loved, valued, and safe. Parents can learn authority and control by commonsense, interpersonal, and practical approaches to day-to-day issues and situations in parenting.

(trade paper)  ISBN 0914984667  **$10.95**

### *God's Abundance*  —Kathy Collard Miller

Subtitled: *365 Days to a Simpler Life.* This day-by-day inspirational is a collection of thoughts by leading Christian writers such as Georgia Burkett, Patsy Clairmont, Corrie ten Boom and Liz Curtis Higgs. *God's Abundance*, is based on God's Word for a simpler, yet more abundant life. Similar in style to the best-seller, *Simple Abundance*, but with a Biblical basis. Learn to make all aspects of your life—personal, business, financial, relationships, even housework be a "spiritual abundance of simplicity."

(hardcover)  ISBN 0914984977  **$19.95**

### *God's Vitamin "C" for the Spirit of WOMEN*  —Kathy Collard Miller

Subtitled: *"Tug-at-the-Heart"* stories to Inspire and Delight Your Spirit. A beautiful treasury of timeless stories, quotes and poetry designed by and for women. Well-known Christian women like Liz Curtis Higgs, Pasty Clairmont, Naomi Rhode and Elisabeth Elliott share from their hearts on subjects like Marriage, Motherhood, Christian Living, Faith and Friendship.

(trade paper)  ISBN 0914984934  **$12.95**

## Purchasing Information:

Listed books are available from your favorite Bookstore, either from current stock or special order. To assist bookstores in locating your selection be sure to give title, author, and 10 digit ISBN #. If unable to purchase from the bookstore you may order direct from STARBURST PUBLISHERS. When ordering, enclose full payment plus $3.00 for shipping and handling ($4.00 if Canada or overseas). Payment in US Funds only. Please allow two to three weeks minimum (longer overseas) for delivery. Make checks payable to and mail to STARBURST PUBLISHERS, P.O. Box 4123, LANCASTER, PA 17604. **Prices subject to change without notice.** Catalog available for a 9 x 12 self-addressed envelope with 4 first-class stamps   5-97